The Transcendent Mind
The Missing Peace in Emotional Wellbeing

Sunita Pattani

J Publishing Company Ltd.

London

A catalogue record for this book is available from the British Library.

ISBN 978-1-907989-06-3

IMPORTANT

This book is not intended as a substitute for medical advice. The intent of this book is to provide general information with regard to the subject matter covered. If medical advice or any other expert advice is needed then the services of an appropriate medical professional should be sought.

Printed in Great Britain

The Transcendent Mind
The Missing Peace in Emotional Wellbeing

Dedicated to my brothers,
Aman & Munraj

All Matter originates and exists only by virtue of a force...We must assume behind this force the existence of a conscious and intelligent mind. This mind is the matrix of all matter.

- Max Planck, Physicist.

Foreword
By
Amit Goswami, Ph. D.

The book you are holding in your hand The Transcendent Mind subtitled The Missing Peace in Emotional Wellbeing delivers. In summary, it shows you how using what the author Sunita Pattani calls your transcendent mind you can effect deeper healing of your emotional wounds, deeper than any conventional psychotherapy. And in so doing, the author has produced, independently of quantum physicists, a very effective introduction of what I would unhesitatingly call quantum psychotherapy.

I will explain. The word transcendent is used in esoteric spiritual traditions, sometimes called mysticism, to connote a domain of reality somehow outside of space and time and yet able to affect happenings inside space and time. Many mysteries! How do we define "outside" space and time? Can we go there and verify its existence? Religions, which popularize the esoteric spiritual teachings, compound the problem by giving names like heaven to this transcendent realm suggesting to the popular mind that it is some sort of place where perfection reigns!

The author introduces the domain of transcendence via empirical data of paranormal phenomenon and near-death experiences. Read the account; it is quite convincing. But the truth is, quantum physics is giving us irrefutable science—both theory and experimental data—to that effect for a hundred years. Why haven't you heard about it? Well, most physicists keep it a well-guarded secret via what is some of the best sophistry since the ancient Greeks. Only recently, in the last couple of decades, the truth about transcendence is gradually leaking out, largely thanks to popular books and the Internet.

The first hint came when the great Niels Bohr discovered the quantum leap: when an electron jumps from one atomic orbit to another it does not go through the intervening space; instead, it does it discontinuously. This discontinuous jump is what Bohr called a quantum leap. But our continuity-prejudiced mind asks: where does the electron go in between?

If you watch the television show Star Trek in any of its multiple incarnations, when the starship enterprise takes the leap from ordinary space-time, it goes to hyperspace of faster-than-light travel; but that is fiction. Truth is stranger than fiction. The quantum leap is instantaneous; wherever the electron goes in whatever form, there it must travel at infinite speed.

Bohr's discovery was circa 1913; twelve years later came the discovery of quantum physics proper and its experimental verification came in 1926. And all heaven should have broken lose ever since. Why? Because quantum physics unambiguously theorizes that all objects are waves of possibility; they become particle of actuality when the experimenter measures it. Where do the waves reside? In the domain of potentiality "outside" space and time? Only this way of explaining makes sense of all the experimental data verifying quantum physics, among the data those of the famous double-slit experiment.

As if sensible physicists needed any more confirmation of transcendence, the deciding confirmation came in a 1982 experiment in Paris by a group of physicists led by Alain Aspect. Aspect's experiment proved that indeed the speed of communication in the domain of potentiality is de facto infinite. In other words, communication is instantaneous. This can be only if no signal is needed for the communication because we know from Einstein's relativity theory that all signals must travel at the speed of light or less.

In quantum lingo, we call this domain of signal-less communication nonlocal. In my own work (reported in the book The Self-Aware Universe), I used what is called the quantum measurement theory to show that this domain of potentiality which ancients called transcendent, that quantum physics calls nonlocal, is consciousness itself. Yes, our consciousness—yours and mine—in its most profound non-ordinary state. Think about it—when you communicate with your self, you don't need a signal do you? So this transcendent domain of potentiality must be one undivided entity—consciousness and its possibilities. Consciousness is the ground in which possibilities exist for all manifest beings—

our experiences. This consciousness is so non-ordinary that it is unconscious in us, so says quantum measurement theory.

The author calls this transcendent domain of our consciousness Transcendent Mind using the old parlance of some spiritual traditions. No matter; whatever name you call the rose.

In order to apply to psychology the concept of transcendent mind or quantum nonlocal consciousness or quantum unconscious—whatever you may want to call it—the author goes ahead and implicitly assumes all our experiences come from the unconscious including those that reflect emotional wounding caused by trauma. Realize that emotion is thought plus feeling.

Now unconscious is of course a familiar term in psychology; it is the great discovery of Sigmund Freud who theorized in the tail end of the nineteenth century that the (personal) unconscious is the container of all the suppressed and repressed trauma of our childhood and later life. The eruptions of these unconscious material gives us neurosis.

Freud's theory of psychoanalysis implies that if we make the unconscious conscious through analysis, we will be healed. But over a hundred years of application has not produced much successful healing. And here the author makes a quantum leap. We need to follow through—psychoanalysis is only part of preparation for a process. This process is designed to access the quantum unconscious. Here the author correctly, like a vintage quantum connoisseur, theorizes that what the mind creates as emotional trauma by giving meaning to a feeling, the key to the healing is not in the meaning-giving mind. Instead, it's in a higher facility that we have that Sri Aurobindo calls the supramental; intuitions and creative insights come from that facility. Intuitions and creative insights are never before manifested quantum possibilities, never before experienced. In other words they are not part of the Freudian unconscious. You cannot access them through analysis. You have go through the process that the author lays out for you discovered through her empirical data of successful therapy that she has taken her patients through.

What is remarkable to me is that the process that the author has empirically discovered is remarkably close to the creative process that creativity researchers and quantum psychologists like me talk about. So congratulations Sunita Pattani for the first definitive book on quantum psychology. You beat me to it and I am delighted. Psychologists and psychotherapists everywhere, take note!

Needless to mention dear reader, the book will keep you spellbound as it did me. Read it, use it for self-help or in conjunction with a therapist, use it for quantum leaps to positive mental health. How far down the rabbit hole of quantum deeper healing do you want to go?

-Amit Goswami (Theoretical Quantum Physicist)

I am a Therapist;

My aim is to help one lessen their emotional suffering, to help one achieve a greater sense of inner peace;

I am not a Scientist and nor am I a Medical Professional;

I do not have all the answers, and neither is my life without obstacles;

I, too have to work on improving aspects of myself, and by doing so I seek to gain a deeper understanding about life;

But…

I recognise my inner calling, and I yield to what life chooses to express through me;

I believe there is an intelligence that exists beyond our body and our ego mind, and not recognising its existence is the source of our suffering.

We do not suffer because life is cruel.

We suffer because we do not realise who we are.

Preface

Last year I received a distressing phone call from a lady who would later go on to become one of my clients. She had found my contact number and was calling me to enquire about counselling sessions. Through tears of desperation, she revealed that she seriously needed some help and that she had attempted suicide twice before. I distinctly remember her asking me to stay on the phone a little longer as she just needed somebody there for her at that moment. As the gentle conversation continued, we scheduled a time to meet. Unfortunately she didn't attend the first few times that we had scheduled, but a couple of months later, she contacted me again to book a session, and this time she came.

During the session she told me about some of the challenges that she was experiencing. She had extremely low self-esteem and was finding it very difficult to forgive and let go of certain situations. She had also had psychiatric help, but nothing had really worked. We started to work together and gradually over the months she started to experience emotional healing. Although the journey was taking time, she was no longer in a place where she would again consider suicide.

We are still working together today and she tells me that she would not have been able to make the change if our sessions didn't explore the very core of who she is. She doesn't believe that she would have healed if she was given *just* conventional psychotherapy. In fact I have worked with hundreds of clients now, and many of them feel the same way.

You see, I believe that the time has now come for us to look beyond just our psychology. Rather than consider psychotherapy from purely a psychological perspective, we now need to give consideration to other disciplines too - such as science and spirituality. For how can we ever heal ourselves properly if we do not know who we are? How can we fill the void of loneliness and learn to forgive others if we do not know about the connection that we share?

I have chosen to write this book because I believe this information needs to be readily available to people who want to heal emotionally. Having witnessed people healing, changing and experiencing more of a deeper meaningful life, I feel that way forward is through awareness of who we really are. Emotional healing isn't just about expressing yourself, exploring your past and changing behaviours, it's also about realising a deeper truth – and for this, we need to look outside of the conventional box.

I hope you find the following chapters both intriguing and inspiring, for it is both my deepest desire and calling to be able to serve you. Only by each one of us making a decision to change will we go on to create a more consciously evolved future generation.

Introduction

She was tired after having worked a long day, but she had still decided to come in for her therapy session. She sat comfortably in the warm, neutrally decorated therapy room, which was quite a contrast to the dark, crisp winter evening on display outside. With questioning eyes and a slightly raised vocal tone, she spoke. *"I don't understand. Why should I consider the bigger picture? What relevance does this have to me? How is it going to help my healing now?"*

I stopped for a moment, paused, trying to organise and collect my thoughts. She had asked a valid question. It wasn't that I didn't have some understanding of the answer, because I'd spent the past thirteen years searching for it myself. It was more a case that I didn't know how to articulate it concisely enough for it to make a difference. Why should she consider the bigger picture? What relevance did it have to her? How was it going to help her healing now?

*

I am a Psychotherapist. My aim is to help individuals attain a greater sense of inner peace and I get to glimpse (very personally), into the lives of others on a daily basis. I observe their pain and obstacles, and in many cases during the process of therapy, I also witness the beginnings of a shift in their consciousness.

I have found that sometimes using the tools and techniques that I have been trained to use are enough to help a client with their issues. But I have also observed in some cases that these approaches alone are not enough to help with emotional healing. It's almost as if the client feels that there's a deeper purpose to life – something they can feel but yet are not able to describe; an inner yearning or even emptiness at times, that they can't quite comprehend.

It's not that these un-named feelings or concepts have not been addressed in the previous psychological theories, but in my opinion, it's rather a case that they are not always fully understood or considered, because they have (what some may refer to as), a mystical element to them.

Having made the choice to continually work on my own personal development, and to explore other areas of research such as parapsychology and near-death experiences, I feel that I have gained a broader perspective on emotional healing. I have personally experienced both shifts in consciousness and glimpses of the truth, and I feel that this has greatly impacted the way in which I work with clients as a Psychotherapist. Had I not have researched the mind from a multidisciplinary perspective, perhaps I may not have further delved into concepts such as Maslow's peak experiences or Jung's notion of collective unconscious. I personally feel that my psychotherapy training alone did not equip me to fully connect with the depth of some of the theories, but rather it has been my personal inquisition into *who I really am* that has gifted me this experience. From a personal perspective, I believe that I can only help my clients to the extent of my own experience and understanding.

I would also like to mention here that I am *not* saying that my choice of method is the *only* way to facilitate emotional healing. Every therapist and client is different and has his or her own methods of working and responding. What I am sharing with you instead, is my own experience of what I have learned through questioning and researching the nature of consciousness and how this relates to emotional healing. I propose that instead of just looking at an individual's challenges and behaviour, we start to ask the all-important question of *'Who Am I?'*

When we start to go beyond observing and managing the ego mind, we begin to realise that we are in fact *not* just this ego mind, but additionally we are something far greater, interconnected with everything else, forming one universal truth. The question, *'Who am I?'* asks that we entertain the notion that we are more than just the body and ego mind. It asks that we expand our awareness about ourselves and perhaps consider the place where psychology and mysticism meet.

1
The Transcendent Mind

An Overview
Where Psychology Meets Mysticism

Let's start off by asking the question of why someone decides to come in for therapy or pursue self-help? It doesn't matter whether one wants a quick fix or whether one wants to learn more about themselves on a deeper level; the reason for pursuing therapy or self-help is to attain a sense of inner peace. Wanting to attain a sense of inner peace implies that on some level, we're thinking thoughts that are causing us to experience a *lack* of inner peace.

When a client comes in for therapy we start to examine what issues they're experiencing and what thoughts and beliefs could be the cause of this lack of inner peace. We consider the present, delve into the client's past and may consider using behavioural modifications techniques to help change their thinking patterns, behaviours and actions.

Despite this, however, for some individuals the issues continue to persist. Sometimes I see people who have an outwardly content lifestyle, but yet they feel a deep sense of emptiness and don't know why. It is these cases (including my own personal suffering) that prompted me to look deeper into why people find it difficult to move past emotional suffering. It's not that individuals don't try; in fact some of them have been very dedicated to their own personal growth, but somehow they still remain stuck.

The combination of my search for answers and my interest in science and spirituality has led me to ask myself some important questions: *How could I move towards healing myself if I didn't have an adequate understanding of who I was? What was my mind and where did my thoughts come from? What connection was there between my mind and my body? And was I anything else aside from the mind and the body?* The findings and concepts that I have come across have gifted me with a realisation that there is a whole different world of discovery going on out there - of which I had previously virtually no clue about. What was even more surprising was that I was beginning to see a link between some of the work that I was discovering, and the work that I was doing with clients.

My biggest shift in perception occurred some time ago when I began reading *A Course in Miracles*. Initially I found it a little daunting as the text used terminology such as 'God' and 'Holy Spirit', and to be honest the last thing that I really wanted to do was to mix psychotherapy with a text that, to me, sounded somewhat religious. There was a big part of me that felt uncomfortable with bringing God into the equation where my work was concerned. This is because I felt that the term 'God' had earned itself an interesting reputation over the years, where it meant different things to different people, and of course was a sensitive topic for some. Quite frankly, I was afraid of being judged and not being taken seriously enough. I was afraid that my clients might be offended or even switch off if God was brought into psychotherapy. However, I knew instinctively that there was something missing from conventional psychotherapy. I felt that it was an inquisitive practice to help an individual become aware and work through their challenges, but it didn't go deep enough. For me personally, psychotherapy didn't consider the existence of our nature seriously enough. Again, if I didn't know who I was at the core, how could I expand my awareness? Did God exist? Who or what was God – an individual entity or a Universal Oneness? And if God (or a Universal Oneness) did exist, what relationship or connection did I have with this Being? What if the answers to these questions were an integral part of my emotional healing?

When I finally did manage to look past the language in *A Course in Miracles*, I soon realised that it was actually a tool to help train our minds and was echoing a lot of the reading that I had already done. What made *A Course in Miracles* different was that it first explained who we were at our very core, and then proceeded with the lessons in how to re-train our minds. I found this combination to be very powerful because it provided an avenue to explore a part of us that went further than just the ego mind. Failing to understand these concepts was the root cause of the emptiness that some of my clients were experiencing.

According to the Course, there is One Mind, which is also referred to as the *Mind of God* or the *Mind of Christ*. The One Mind has been split into individual minds, hence creating separate human beings. Our individual minds are further split into two parts: *Spirit* and *ego*.

The Spirit, which is sometimes referred to as "soul", is considered to be the Thought of God, created by Him in His own image. This is the part of us that is still in contact with our Creator and, it is also the part of us that has the potential to create. The Spirit speaks the truth to us very gently, and when we're displaying *right-mindedness*, we're following that guidance. [1]

The ego is the part of us that is *illusionary*. It is the part of us that has us believe that we're separate. The ego doesn't recognise that we're actually deeply interconnected and are an integral part of the universe. Obviously, we have separate bodies and individual minds, but we are also part of something much greater. When we believe that we are nothing other than our separate selves, it can be easy to be selfish, angry, greedy and inconsiderate towards those around us. After all, what motivation do we have to be loving towards one another? Instead we take the attitude that this is our life and that we need to do whatever we can to survive. Rather than coming together and collaborating with one another, we choose the path of competition. A world that believes itself to be made up of separate beings not connected in any way, is a world that finds it hard to forgive and move on. It is also a world that operates on the basis of conditional love. How can a world with this belief system possibly create a truly peaceful existence?

I have to admit that I found this concept of a transcendent, unified mind difficult to accept at first. I questioned how we were all interconnected because to me, we all seemed individual, we all had free choice, and as far as I knew, our individual thoughts were private. I also questioned the concept of "God." What or who was God? I had never really resonated with the idea of an old man with a long white beard sitting in the clouds, looking down at us and judging our every move. But I did believe that there was something greater than us out there, and that our personal existence wasn't just down to chance.

As I started to research more about interconnectedness and who we were at the core, I found that not only had this concept been written about, but there was also research to suggest that interconnectedness was real – that perhaps a Transcendent Mind existed. Up until then I had only been familiar with Freud's notion of the mind.

Freud stated that there were three levels of mind: *conscious, preconscious* and *unconscious.* The conscious mind is the part of us that is aware. It is the part of us that is able to think and speak rationally. The preconscious mind stores thoughts and memories that we may not be consciously thinking of, but are able to easily bring into awareness if we choose. For example, we may not be consciously thinking about our phone number but we are able to recall and bring it into conscious awareness. The unconscious mind according to Freud, is the largest part of our mind. It stores our childhood memories, our instincts and any traumatic events that we may have experienced. These memories are not part of our conscious awareness and may have been deliberately forgotten. They do however; still continue to influence our behaviour and actions.[2]

Although some of Freud's (psychodynamic) theory was considered controversial, the idea that our thoughts and behaviour stem from our unconscious mind, was regarded by many scholars as revolutionary. Psychologist Carl Jung was one such person who was influenced by Freud's work and is hence referred to as a *Neo-Freudian.* However, Jung did go on to develop his own theory, which included the concept of the *collective unconscious.* Jung claimed that the collective unconscious is common to us all, and is not something that we develop, but instead is something that we inherit. According to Jung, the collective unconscious includes the totality of human history that we all have access to and contains archetypes and universal ideas.[3]

Whilst the behaviourist and psychodynamic approaches were dominant during the first half of the twentieth century, the second half of the twentieth century saw the development of the humanistic approach, with Psychologists Carl Rogers and Abraham Maslow's views central to this area. This approach was about understanding one's subjective experience and asking the important question of "Who am I?" The notion that people are *basically good* was also a prominent theme of this approach, with Carl Rogers believing that human beings had an innate tendency to move towards growth and positive change. He labelled this basic motivating force an *actualizing tendency.*

Abraham Maslow places self-actualization at the top of his *Hierarchy of Needs*. Maslow's hierarchy of needs outlines seven needs, with the most basic biological needs at the bottom (such as food and shelter), moving to the more complex psychological needs (such as self-actualization) at the top. Maslow claimed that the basic needs had to first be at least partially met before the higher needs could be fulfilled. During his lifetime Maslow also studied *self-actualizers* – people who he felt had used their potential well, in an attempt to identify the traits and behaviours displayed by these individuals.[4]

Whilst researching for this book, I commonly came across Maslow's hierarchy of needs and some information about his concept of *peak experiences*. However, feeling that I was in need of a better understanding about some of his concepts, I decided to read his book, *Religions, Values and Peak experiences*, (1970). What I found most interesting was that he recognised the multidisciplinary aspect of psychology. In other words, he knew that people had subjective, internal experiences and gave consideration to these. He also felt that there wasn't enough consideration given to the *spiritual* or *higher* aspects of life.

Maslow felt that we had to redefine both science and religion as both of these disciplines had become too pigeonholed and separated from one another. Nineteenth century science, he felt, had become too mechanistic and free from spiritual values, whereas religion was not accepting of facts and scientific knowledge. Rather than be viewed as dichotomised, it was thought that these two disciplines should be used to strengthen one another. Maslow expressed that it was perfectly acceptable to be asking religious questions, as this was an inquiry into the roots of human nature, and he also felt that these could be studied and examined in a scientific manner. (Maslow, 1970)

From a personal perspective, perhaps one of the most interesting concepts that Maslow studied was something that he termed as *peak experiences*. These were regarded as mystical illuminations, transcendent experiences or revelations. These were usually individual experiences where one discovered their truth about themselves, God and the world.

It was first thought that only some people had these peak-experiences, but in time and through further research Maslow realised that everyone had these peak experiences, and those who didn't were either afraid or in denial about them. He used the term "non-peakers" to describe people who fell into this category. It was also noted that these individuals were of an extreme rational type and mechanistic in nature.[5]

I have personally experienced brief moments of these peak states in the past. I remember one day around ten years ago when I was taking a walk in the park. For a few seconds I felt a really warm, tingling sensation, and almost excited feeling in my body and at that moment I knew I was connected to something divine. Although I cannot fully describe my experience in words, I felt a deep sense of connectedness – a knowing that everything was going to be ok. I felt on some level that there was more to me than just my body.

The interesting thing that I have found about these experiences is that they were spontaneous and unpredictable in their occurrence. They weren't something that I could "will" or "think" into happening, but rather they occurred at their own pace. For me, they were glimpses of universal truth.

These experiences can be difficult to study because of the nature of their existence. We study a concept from a logical, objective perspective and we try to understand, rationalise and explain certain phenomena. However, these experiences cannot always be rationalised, or even understood by someone solely from an intellectual perspective. Although one may not be able to find the right language to describe the experience, or even understand its precise mechanism, the individual knows instinctively that there is a deeper truth. Metaphorically speaking, this is not something that is experienced in the mind; it is experienced in the heart.

The interesting thing to consider is that people from all walks of life have documented these experiences throughout the centuries. They aren't specific to any race, religion or sex, but rather they seem to be a universal occurrence, capable of being experienced by anybody. Maslow (1970) makes an important point in saying that organized religion has come about because of one person having experienced this deep truth – a peak-experience. Religion aims to communicate this peak experience to "non-peakers", however this is often a difficult task as the communicators themselves may be "non-peakers". In other words, the information is intellectualised and the true meaning may be lost.

When I first started reading *A Course in Miracles*, I realised that it had been "scribed" (through a process of inner dictation), by two Psychologists: Dr. Helen Schucman and Dr. William Thetford. Therefore, it seemed natural for me to start my journey of exploration through the field of psychology. I soon realised however, that it wasn't just Psychologists and Theologians that had referred to "interconnectedness" and a "greater intelligence", but in fact, some scientists too had talked about these concepts, for example, the famous 20th Century Physicist Max Planck stated:

> *"As a man who has devoted his whole life to the most clear headed science, to the study of matter, I can tell you as a result of my research about atoms this much: There is no matter as such. All matter originates and exists only by virtue of a force which brings the particle of an atom to vibration and holds this most minute solar system of the atom together. We must assume behind this force the existence of a conscious and intelligent mind."* [6]

In the past hundred years or so, we have become familiar with certain terminology connected with the mind. Terms such as the *conscious, preconscious, unconscious* and *collective consciousness* have been introduced to us. Understanding more about the way in which our personal mind works has been an important milestone in facilitating emotional healing. For example, recognising that some of our behaviour may be the result of past experiences that haven't been internally resolved, tells us what we need to work on. However, although extremely beneficial, knowing who we are as individuals is only part of the truth, and if we only know ourselves partially, how can we understand and experience a deeper healing?

Susan came to me for therapy after spending four weeks in rehab to deal with an alcohol addiction. Although she was no longer drinking, she did have other issues that she wanted to address. When I asked her how she had finally managed to stop drinking, she told me that she believed that her body was a temple that was housing her inner being - her spirit. This realisation had prompted her to treat her body with the respect that it deserved. I noticed that Susan was hesitating slightly as she was telling me about her breakthrough. When I asked her why this was the case, she told me that her previous therapist had not understood what she had meant when she referred to her body as temple. The therapist had told Susan that she was a little concerned about this analogy, and this of course had made Susan feel uncomfortable and in her own words, "a little silly."

Although I am sure that Susan's therapist was very good, this example does highlight the need that we have to have a better understanding about ourselves. The fact of the matter is that many of us, at some time or another, feel that there is more to us than meets the eye – and just like in Susan's case, these feelings or revelations can very often help us with our own emotional healing. As well as looking at ourselves on a personal level, we now need to question where we fit in the grander scheme of things.

This book is about the grander scheme of things. In the recent years we have seen studies exploring concepts such as telepathy and psychic phenomena. We have also heard stories from all around the world about people who talk about both near death and out-of-body experiences, some of whom have experienced revelations of what they consider to be the truth. This evidence suggests the existence of a deeper dimension – an integral part of ourselves that cannot necessarily be seen, but rather is something that we experience. Therefore this book explores the concept of a *Transcendent Mind: a Mind that not only goes beyond our individual minds, but also includes our personal, individualised minds. The Transcendent Mind is common to us all and is responsible for the experience of interconnectedness. It is an all-pervading consciousness, that has the ability to transcend time and space. This part of us that we need to re-acknowledge and become aware of, for it is this part of us that knows the truth about who we really are.*

I believe the time has come that we recognise the limitations of the conscious mind in relation to emotional healing; and that we begin to open up to the notion that there is a part of us that transcends our current perception of the mind. Indeed civilization is now stood at perhaps one of the most crucial junctions ever, where the dichotomies of ancient spiritualism and modern research appear to be merging, where the truth shall finally set us free.

Part One

The Transcendent Mind
Experiences

2
The Infinite Transcendent Mind

For the soul there is never birth nor death. Nor, having once been, does he ever cease to be. He is unborn, eternal, ever-existing, undying and primeval. He is not slain when the body is slain.

-The Bhagavad Gita (Chapter 2, Verse 20.)

In the last chapter, I stated that the Transcendent Mind *is a Mind that not only goes beyond our individual minds, but also includes our personal, individualised minds too. It is common to us all and is responsible for the experience of interconnectedness. The Transcendent Mind is an all-pervading consciousness that has the ability to transcend time and space.* In the following chapters I am going to be expanding on this explanation by sharing with you additional aspects of the Transcendent Mind and how we personally experience it. This chapter is about the *infinite, omnipresent and omniscient* nature of the Transcendent Mind.

Whilst researching the eternal nature of the Transcendent Mind, I frequently came across people referring to the Vedas or the Bhagavad Gita – sacred texts that form the foundation of Hinduism. Albert Einstein (1879-1955) once said, *"When I read the Bhagavad Gita and reflect about how God created this Universe, everything else appears superfluous".*[1] The famous American poet and philosopher Henry David Thoreau (1817-1862) has also referred to the Bhagavad Gita, saying, *"In the morning I bathe my intellect in the stupendous and cosmological philosophy of the Bhagavad Gita, in comparison with which our modern world and literature seem puny and trivial."*[2]

As I started to study the Bhagavad Gita, I realised that its definition of the Soul was similar to that given in *A Course in Miracles*. In the last chapter I referred to *A Course in Miracles*, which introduced the concept of the "One Mind." The One Mind is considered to be the Mind of God, which has been split into our individual minds. The individual mind is further split into two components: the ego and the Spirit. The ego is the part of us that sees us as being separate from one another and, the Spirit is the part of us that has the potential to create and provide us with an inner guidance. The Spirit also knows that we are all interconnected.

The Bhagavad Gita also refers to an all-pervading consciousness called *Brahman*. Brahman manifests in a number of different ways, including: *Ishvara*, Supreme Godhead; *Jivas*, living entities, *Prakriti*, material nature and the eternal concept of time.[3]

I see both concepts of *One Mind* and *Brahman* to mean the same thing – *the Transcendent Mind*. According to the Bhagavad Gita, we as Human Beings are referred to as the living entities, *Jivas*. It is stated that although we have an individual consciousness, we also have a localised aspect of the Supreme Soul within our hearts. In other words, we have both the Transcendent Mind and the ego within us.

This can be a difficult concept to understand because it seems almost paradoxical. If the Transcendent Mind is the ground of all being, a universal consciousness that gives rise to all, then how can we still be individual? How can we be a manifestation of the Transcendent Mind and yet be separate from it? This is best understood through the following example: Imagine the ocean to be the Transcendent Mind, and now imagine yourself to be a single droplet of the ocean. Being a single droplet of that ocean, you still possess all the qualities of the whole ocean such as being the same consistency and being salty in taste. However, although you possess these qualities, you are not the whole ocean. In this way, you are both a manifestation of the Transcendent Mind, possessing its qualities, but you are also individual, standing independent.[4]

The Upanishads[1] illustrate how these two components, the Transcendent Mind and the ego, operate within us: There are two birds, both friends and companions sitting on a tree. One of the birds is eating the fruit off the tree, hopping from branch to branch engaging in the different tastes of the fruit. The sweet fruit brings him joy and the bitter fruit brings discomfort. This bird experiences anxiety and moroseness.

The other bird sat on a higher branch is in a state of calm and peace, and silently witnesses what is happening. He is unmoved by the temptation of the fruit on the tree.

One day the fruit-eating bird looks up and sees his friend, and is immediately attracted to his peaceful nature. With his attention on his peaceful friend, the fruit-eating bird becomes free from his anxieties.[5]

Metaphorically speaking, both birds reside within the human being. The fruit-eating bird represents the ego mind whose happiness is dependent upon the material world and changing circumstances. This part of us experiences stress and anxieties based on what is happening in our external environment.

The peaceful bird represents the Transcendent Mind, which is always there in the background, silently witnessing all that is happening, unmoved by the changing circumstances that life brings. The Transcendent Mind is able to absorb anxiety and grief if we chose to shift our internal attention toward it.

According to the Bhagavad Gita, we as livings entities are a manifestation of the Supreme Consciousness - the Transcendent Mind, which is described as being infinite and omnipresent. Therefore, it is said that we too possess these qualities. A fundamental question for us to be asking is how we experience this infinite aspect of the Transcendent Mind. If we are both part of, and connected to this universal web that appears to be infinite, then there must be an aspect of us that continues to exist even once we die, and if this is the case then what happens to us once we die?

Near-death Experiences

Near-death and out-of-body experiences are avenues that we can consider to help give us some perspective on this phenomenon. Let's first start

---

1   The Upanishads are the central scriptures of Hinduism. The story of the two birds is told in chapter three of the Mundaka Upanishad

off by exploring the term *near-death experience*. According to the International Association for Near Death Studies (IANDS), in 1975, Dr. Raymond Moody first used the term *near death experience* in his book *Life After Life*.[2]

A near-death episode is usually experienced when the person is either clinically dead or in a situation where they are likely to die, for example during a suicide attempt or serious illness. IANDS describe a near-death experience (NDE) as *"a distinct subjective experience that people sometimes report after a near-death episode."* Most individuals who have undergone an NDE have felt that the experience was very real.[6]

Although unique to individuals, NDEs do share some common characteristics. These characteristics include for example, a feeling of being out of one's body (where consciousness detaches itself from the physical body); encountering deceased loved ones or saintly figures (such as Jesus); gaining information about universal secrets; travelling through darkness or a tunnel and, having a life review where the individual experiences all their actions as well as the impact that these actions have had on other people. In some cases, individuals report that they have made the choice to return back to their physical bodies.[7]

As part of the research for this book I interviewed NDE Researcher, Dr. Penny Sartori who used to work as a Nurse in an intensive care unit. She told me of an incident where she was nursing a patient one night who was clearly going to die. During this time she made a connection with the patient and when the patient died the following day, Penny found herself falling into a deep depression. In order to try and understand more about the death process, she started to read about the subject and came across near-death experiences. Penny was quite surprised to find that lots of people who had had these experiences were saying that death was nothing to be afraid of.

Penny started to question what near-death experiences were – were they just hallucinations, or were they a real phenomenon? And with this curiosity in mind, she conducted her own study that focussed on exploring the experiences of survivors who had suffered a cardiac arrest. During our interview, Penny shared the following:

---

2   It should however be noted that many people who have been through a near-death experience feel that the term "near-death" is not an accurate term to be using as these individuals believe that they were actually dead during the episode.

Out of 39 patients, 7 of them reported an NDE and I found them to be of varying quality as well. In fact for some of them, it didn't really have much significance for the person, yet they clearly experienced elements or components of an NDE. The person didn't understand it, so they didn't attach any significance; they just put it to the back of their mind.

Some of them had quite deep experiences as well. There was one case of a man who had an out of body experience (OBE), where he proceeded into another room where he met his dead father and a Jesus-like figure. During the OBE, he also reported the actions of the Nurse, the Doctor and the Physiotherapist, and he was very accurate with what he described, and I know he was accurate because I was there. I was the Nurse looking after him. However at the time he was deeply unconscious. He hadn't had a cardiac arrest, so his heart was still beating, but he was deeply unconscious, and what he reported was correct.

Following the experience, another interesting aspect transpired. Now, this patient had cerebral palsy, and so his right hand had been in a permanently contracted position from birth. After his experience, when I was interviewing him, he misinterpreted one of my questions. I had said to him, 'when you were out of your body, was there anything that you could do that you can't normally do?' And what I meant by that was that some people feel that when they have an OBE and when they think of a particular location, they will find themselves there, and that's what I was getting at. But he misinterpreted that and said, "oh yeah, look at my hand, I can open it out." And he went on to open out his hand fully - and he's never been able to do that before. At first I didn't realise the significance of this, but when I discussed it with the Doctor and with the Physiotherapist, they said that this shouldn't be possible because he'd have to have an operation to release the tendons in order to open up the hand. Well, nothing like that was done and yet this man could fully open out his hand.[8]

Perhaps one of the most compelling experiences that I have ever come across is the one of Anita Moorjani. Anita is the author of *Dying to be Me*, who had a profound near-death experience. Suffering with end stage cancer, (Hodgkin's Lymphoma), Anita was rushed into hospital when she fell into a coma in February 2006. Her family were told that her organs were shutting down and that she was unlikely to make it through the next thirty-six hours. However, during this time of being in a coma Anita was aware of everything that was going on around her. She could see and hear the conversations taking place between her husband and the doctors who were 40 feet away down the hallway – a conversation that her husband was later able to verify.

She also experienced crossing over to another dimension where she was *engulfed* totally in the feeling of love. She gained an understanding of how life generally worked and she also understood why she had the cancer. Anita knew why she had come into this life and what role her family were playing in the grander scheme of things. She realised that she had a choice of returning to her physical body or choosing death, however, she was told that it was not yet her time and if she chose death she would not experience the gifts that life yet had to offer. She was also aware that if she chose to come back, she would heal very quickly.

Making the choice to come back, Anita recovered rapidly from the cancer – much to her doctors' surprise! She now travels the world sharing her experience with others, bringing knowledge, comfort and guidance to them[3].

Kelly Walsh, founder of *Positivity Princess* is on a mission to create a global community of children and adults that incorporate love, caring and sharing into their daily lives. Kelly shares her experience:

Like a lot of children I was bullied for being overweight, and as a result I felt 'different' - as if I was a misfit. Outwardly I appeared happy with a big smile on my face, but inwardly I lacked self-love and suffered with self-esteem issues, and eventually at the age of sixteen my low self-esteem resulted in an eating disorder.

---

3   You can learn more about Anita and her amazing story by visiting the website www.anitamoorjani.com

When I turned nineteen, I met my ex-husband who was extremely good looking and I couldn't believe that he found me attractive. I fell in love and life started to get better, however I still had issues that I needed to work on. We eventually got engaged and then married. He was a good man but we had differing views on the world, and spiritually, I felt that we were not aligned. I think looking back I felt trapped, and I started to suffer with periods of deep depression.

At the age of thirty-three I decided I could no longer stay in our marriage and left my husband. As it happens he had already met someone special so it was for the best. Leaving my husband started a sequence of events and over a period of six months I became single, lost my home, lost my job, my granddad died and I was in a mess financially. Unable to pay my bills, I had to move back in with my parents. I felt so low and didn't know how to cope. I had lost all hope. Shortly afterwards, somebody passed a comment that I felt was the last straw and I decided to end my life. I grabbed all the tablets in the medical cupboard and swallowed them. I then wrote a note and put it with the empty packets under my pillow so they would not be found until I was hopefully dead. I got a friend to pick me up and asked her to drop me off with another friend and called my mum that night and said I was staying at my friends for a couple of days. She had no reason to suspect otherwise.

I could not believe it when next day I awoke and was still alive so I got my friend to buy me a packet of tablets (obviously she had no idea why), and again swallowed the lot. Three days later I was still alive and couldn't believe it - but my skin was starting to scratch and I was coughing up bile. That night nearly seventy-two hours after taking the first lot of tablets I spoke to my mum and something clicked. I told my friend what I had done and she rushed me to the hospital. Blood tests were taken and when the doctor came back in you could see the look of horror on his face. My liver enzymes were at 10, 000 when they should be at 40,000 and I had in excess of 20, 000 milligrams of paracetamol in my body. They couldn't pump my stomach, as too many days had passed since I had taken the *tablets and my organs were starting to shut down. I was taken into an observation ward and was put on a drip.*

I remember feeling fearful that I was going to burn in hell for committing the cardinal sin. There was a Gideon bible on the side of my bed and started to read it at what seemed like a hundred miles per hour. Next morning a beautiful nurse who had white blonde hair touched my arm and the only words she spoke were, "when you get out of here, read the book Conversations with God", and then she vanished. (I have since been told that book by Neale Donald Walsch comes into your life when it supposed to.)

At this stage however, I was still fearful and I sent for the onsite minister to pray over me. When he arrived he gave me a small wooden cross. The following night I had what I can only describe as a near-death experience. It was night-time and I was holding onto my wooden cross and I was pumping with sweat. I felt like there were spiritual beings around me with their fingers over their mouths as if to say keep quiet. I felt as if I was travelling on a journey through bumps and dimensions in the universe. As I travelled, my whole life flashed before me. It wasn't in any particular order - all sort of jumbled up. I did not find this a pleasant experience and it actually felt like a battle to survive. Eventually I travelled through seven dimensions to the other side and all of a sudden, I felt a wave of relief come over me. I felt as if I had 'made it' and I really felt at peace. Then, I remember someone having a conversation with me and I was told I was strong, which seemed ironic considering what I had just done. I was told I had work to carry out on earth and was shown that as humans, we have the capacity to heal physically, emotionally and spiritually through LOVE. It was demonstrated to me that we are all one, all connected. They,(to be honest I don't know who they were), told me I could be and do anything I wanted.

In the week to follow, I left hospital in good health – which is a miracle considering the amount of pills that I had ingested. I also received a vision that I had to help change the world by collaborating with others.[9]

The individuals in the above case studies although deeply unconscious, were still alive when they had their experience. Even though these cases display some remarkable, unexplainable happenings, such as Anita's miraculous recovery or the gentleman with cerebral palsy who can now open his hand, some sceptics would still suggest that there is a logical explanation for the occurrence of the NDEs/OBEs. [10]

However, there are also people that have had NDEs whilst being clinically dead. In an interview with the Author of *Lessons in Courage*, don Oscar Miro-Quesada, I learned that he had experienced two near death experiences. The first one took place in 1961 when he was ten years old. Don Oscar suffered with chronic asthma during his childhood, and one night, a short while after his mother had put him to sleep, don Oscar found himself awake and unable to breathe. Although he tried desperately to call for help, he found himself unable to move or speak. He could feel the world closing in on him as his heartbeat became fainter and fainter until it was no longer present. Don Oscar had died.

In this state, he could somehow hear his nickname (Beaver) being called from a far distance, "Beaver, Beaver, come back. We need you." He then felt himself return to his bed, sitting upright in complete darkness. As he started to regain consciousness, he felt the presence of indescribable compassion, grace, love and healing, and as he looked on in the darkness, he witnessed three human-like forms appear. They were seven feet tall and dressed in long white robes. Through thought communication with the three beings, don Oscar recognised his true essence, and although he knew that he could have chosen not to come back, he also felt that it was not yet his time to die. One of the beings then healed don Oscar's asthma. After this happened, he was shown more about his life, including the jobs that he would hold, the relationships that he would treasure and the teachers that he would meet. He was also shown what he was here to do as service to life, and knew that the asthma was gone forever.

The second NDE took place when Don Oscar was thirty-three years old. One evening in a state of frustration, he took to the road in his car. With the aim of ending his life, he experienced a car crash. As he regained consciousness after the crash he found himself still in the driver's seat with blood pouring out of his head where he had hit the steering wheel. Although he couldn't see anything, he could hear voices and feel people going through his pockets, taking some of his belongings, including his wallet. He could hear them saying that he was dead. He then heard a woman (who had seen the thieves), shouting that someone should call the police.

Don Oscar could feel himself drifting back towards consciousness and he could hear the laughter of little children. Realising that his car was in a different place – quite far from where he had thought he was, don Oscar started to panic, and it was then that he heard a voice in his head telling him to take deep breaths and relax. As he followed these instructions, he could feel himself leaving his body, with all his anxiety and suffering vanishing. He could feel himself being drawn towards a tunnel and was shown images of his daughter living without him and his parents on their knees. He was then shown another place that he described as paradise. This place was free from suffering and full of love. Don Oscar realised that this was a choice.

He then met a being who explained that don Oscar was dead and it was his choice of whether he wanted to stay or return to his human community that still needed him. After being asked about his concept of God and whether he thought it was possible to remain at peace regardless of the external circumstances, don Oscar recognised that it made no difference whether he was alive or dead as it was all part of the universal web. Within this great cosmic ocean, all people were passers-by.

And so don Oscar chose to return to his body, and as he did, he knew that he was perceived as being dead on the Earthly realm. The police had thrown a sheet over his body and taken him to the police station. Although he wasn't sure how much time had passed, he could feel himself re-entering his body, with the blood-flow being restored back to normal. He remembers the sheet falling away as he sat up, with everyone in the room shocked as to how he was alive. [11]

In 2001, The Lancet published a study about near death experiences in survivors of cardiac arrest. This was a prospective study[4] carried out in the Netherlands by Dr. Pim Van Lommel et al. The study found that 18% of

---

4   A prospective study is a study that moves forward in time. It identifies a group of people and follows them over a period of time to see if the outcome of interest takes place.

people had memory from the time of their clinical death, and of these patients, 12% of them had a core NDE[5]. It was also found that the individuals that had undergone the NDE experience became more empathetic, with most of them believing in an afterlife, as well as no longer being fearful of death.[12]

Exploring NDEs in survivors of cardiac arrest is important because of the physiological changes that people go through during the process. A cardiac arrest is when the heart stops beating. When this happens an individual loses consciousness within seconds and both breathing and blood flow to the brain ceases. Within around 10-15 seconds, the brain' s electrical activity stops and hence the brain stops functioning. In an interview with Lilou Mace, Dr. Pim Van Lommel stated,

> *"There's still the assumption that consciousness is a product of the brain function, so when patients have a cardiac arrest and the brain doesn't function anymore after 10 to 15 seconds, it shouldn't be possible that the patients have conscious experience and memories because, the structures that underpin those kind of experiences don't function anymore, as there's no blood flow to the brain"[13]*

In another case study published on the International Association for Near-Death Studies' website, an anonymous individual writes:

> *After having flu-like symptoms for three days, I realized that I was not getting better and tried to find help where I worked. I was alone in London. On reaching work they immediately called a taxi, which took me to the nearest emergency hospital. On arrival I passed out at once and awoke hours later in an isolation ward. Several nurses were washing me down with ice-cold water and forcing me to drink iced water. The windows were wide open in the middle of winter. A doctor arrived and told them to stop, as I was dead. At once, my spirit left my*

---

5   Through researching a number of case studies Dr. Raymond Moody put together a common set of elements that may occur during an NDE – regardless of one's gender, age or culture. These elements are termed 'core experiences'.

body and I looked down and observed the whole scene from above. I could see the nurses had defied the doctor; he slammed the door upon leaving the room.

Almost at once I began a terrifying journey down a black spiral tunnel to an amazingly bright light, the likes I have never seen before or since. On arriving in a very beautiful place, I was met by my mother who had died two years earlier. She told me this was heaven and began to introduce me to family who had died and I had never known. There was a bright light there that I could not look at because of its brightness. After about twenty minutes a man who I did not know came up and told me, "it's not your time yet and you have to go back."

The journey back was the same, but this time into darkness. When I re-entered my body I was in great pain. I was unconscious for around three days. When I finally came to, I was told about having suffered double pneumonia and surviving a temperature of over 108. They said to date no one had ever survived such a high body temperature. After two weeks in the hospital, I was transferred to a convalescent home for an additional two weeks.

The events are as clear in my mind as if they had happened yesterday. I have told many people about my story and some have said it brought great comfort to them.[14]

Blind individuals who have suffered a near-death experience are also another fascinating group of people to consider. A study published in the Journal of Near-Death Studies (1997), sought to explore near-death and out-of-body experiences in the blind. The study conducted by Ring & Cooper found that NDEs in the blind do occur and that they tend to experience the same elements as those of sighted people who have NDEs. These elements amongst others included: travelling through a tunnel, separation from the physical body and encountering the light.

Surprisingly, the study also found that 80% of the respondents claimed to have had visual impressions during the NDE or OBE, and often provided accurate detailed descriptions of what they "saw". However, when questioned further about the nature of their "vision" during these NDEs, it was found that they didn't just experience ordinary vision as we know it, but rather they described having access to a kind of *super sensory* awareness:

> *In summary, what we learned from our respondents is that although their experiences may sometimes be expressed in a language of vision, a close reading of their transcripts suggests something closer to a multifaceted synesthetic perception that seems to involve much more than a physical sight. This is not to say that as part of this awareness there cannot be some sort of pictorial image as well; it is only to assert that this must not be taken in any simplistic way as constituting vision as we normally understand it. (Ring & Cooper, 1997:136)* [15]

The study highlighted that although the blind may not have "seen" in the way that we would normally understand vision; they did appear to experience some sort of an *expanded super-sensory awareness*. Based on this finding, the researchers argued that the blind, just like others who experienced NDEs and OBEs, entered into a *transcendental awareness* – a state of consciousness which was not normally experienced in one's normal waking state.

This study is particularly interesting because the respondents appear to have experienced sight during their NDE. The study itself includes some fascinating case studies that the authors have taken time to corroborate to the best of their ability. (Please refer to the bibliography for the full reference of this study.)

Unable to Move On

(The individual sharing this experience chose to remain anonymous; therefore I will refer to him as "J" throughout the following paragraphs).

In 2002 J and a few of his relatives had first-hand experience of witnessing the spirit world[6]. J belonged to the Hindu faith and as mentioned

---

6   It should be noted that this extract is not only a recollection of an event that took place 12 years ago. The event was documented by J in his personal diary on the day that it happened, and I have personally seen this entry. I have also spoken to the other people who were present independently.

earlier, members of the Hindu faith believe that the soul moves on once the body dies. When a member of the Hindu faith passes away, certain ceremonies and rituals are conducted to ensure that the individual's soul moves on with ease.

In this particular case, J's uncle had passed away back in 1984 and through a religious séance eighteen years later, the family was informed that the uncle had not passed on properly as the ceremonies were not conducted properly. J recalls:

In 1984, my Dad's eldest brother died. He drowned in the sea near his village. They (the family) did his final rites quickly afterwards, but they weren't done properly for some reason. His eldest son was away and there was some unfinished business. For many Hindus, when they die, they expect a transition process and when this process isn't conducted properly, there's a good chance that their soul won't move on properly. They then try to get the family's attention in order for the ceremony to be conducted properly.

So, the funeral was all done. Now fast-forward to the year 2002- every few months or so, we have a séance gathering where we would summon one of our Demi-Goddesses. We call her a "Kur-devi" and she watches over our community. You can call on her anytime that you need to speak to her, and there's usually a channel that brings her forth. And so, we channelled this Demi-Goddesses energy and she brought a message forward specifically for my Dad. The message was, "your elder brother is still here. He is stuck and he can't move on. He requires you to come and finish the final rights for him."

The channel by the way, knew nothing about my uncle. In fact, she knew nothing about our family. So she passed on the message and it seemed that for that entire period between 1984 and 2002, he'd (my deceased uncle), had been getting in the way of a lot of things. For example, my Dad's other brother who lived in India was trying to settle over in the USA and his application just wasn't going through. Also, various business ventures were failing. He wasn't trying to be vindictive, but he was trying to get their attention because he knew they were spiritual and that at some point they would seek advice as to why these things were going wrong – since that's what they had done in the past. But funnily enough, they didn't seek advice this time – they didn't think to ask about those things.

So in 2002, we went to a very old temple called Somnath. The foundations of this temple go back to the time of the Mahabharata, to Krishna's time – we're talking around 5000B.C. It seems like there's a hub of energy there, if that makes sense? Because a lot of people go and do final rights ceremonies there for their relatives that have passed. When you're there you can hear priests channelling spirits or sounds of devastation from some of the rooms. It was a bit unsettling actually.

We started the ceremony quite early – around 6am.It was made up of the initial calling, the summoning and the appeasing. The appeasing part of the ceremony is where you give your offering to the various Demigods, which then allow the spirit to come through so that we can hear him. This took the best part of around five or six hours. After this, we were all sitting there in meditation and waiting for my uncle to come through – but we weren't sure who would come through, whether it would be the priest or someone else. After a short while, I saw my dad's other elder brother beginning to sway back and forth as he was relaxing to see if he would be able to channel his deceased brother. At this point, one of his children (my cousin), recognised that her dad may be going into trance and pulled him out as his health wasn't in top form.

There were actually two mediums with us that were from Mumbai. They were independent and didn't know the family. They weren't aware of what had happened. They were husband and wife. So, after the spirit tried to come through my uncle, it then passed on to the male medium but didn't stay with him for too long. The wife however opened up her hair. The belief is that open hair is like an open portal for the spirit to enter. Within a few seconds of opening up her hair, tears were streaming down her eyes and she was sobbing uncontrollably – and this was his (my uncle's) energy. Through the sobbing, he explained that he had arrived and had received all the offerings, and that he was happy that he could finally move on. We all in turn paid our respects to him and every one of his brothers spoke to him.

Although my Dad and his brothers were quite happy with the outcome, the priest actually stepped in and asked the spirit, "No wait. Who are you?" To which the spirit answered the question. The priest then asked him to prove that he was my uncle. So the priest asked questions such as, "how did you die? Where did you die? Who were you with? What actually happened on the day? At first, my uncle refused to answer the questions as he said that the spirit rule was that he couldn't affect the course of destiny for anyone else, so he wasn't allowed to give that much information away.

In the end they reasoned with him and explained that we couldn't let him go without knowing whether we had made the offerings to the right person. My uncle's spirit then verified exactly what day and what time he died as well as who was with him and how he got pulled under a current, was unable to swim and drowned. He then thanked us and told us that we owed him a glass of water. He told us that as soon as we gave him the glass of water, he could go.

Just as we were about to give him the water, the priest intervened again and told his assistant to go and get water from the sea. The water from the sea was not fit for human consumption and the priest was making sure that the channel was really in a trance. The channel did drink the whole pot of water and remained unaffected.

My uncle's spirit then moved on. After a short while, the Demigoddess then came through again and said that she could see him passing over properly now. This was a really scary experience for me, but it left no doubt in my mind the power of certain rituals if expected by the dying individual. Also, shortly afterwards things started to work out for my Dad and his brothers. His elder brother finally managed to settle down in America. [16]

Shared Death Experiences

Whilst conducting my research, I also came across shared death experiences. This is where an individual who is closely connected to a person dying shares an NDE with them. Jeremy McDonald, author of *Peace Be Still*, had a shared death experience with his mother when she passed away. Jeremy says:

A few days before Christmas we found out that my mother had uterine cancer. We didn't really know until January the 7th 2012 that she wasn't going to make it and that the cancer was actually at stage 4. On January 9th 2012 she passed away.

Why this is exceptional is that she had had an NDE when she suffered a heart attack, two years prior to her passing. She survived the heart attack came back because during that NDE an angel came to her and told her that it wasn't yet her time and that she still had work to do. During the following two years that followed, she resolved all of her things that she needed to let go of, so that she could have a peaceful transition, including the relationship between us. We had a good relationship but it was very co-dependent and during those two years, we went from son and mother to friends.

My mother was a hospice nurse. The night before she died I was told not to leave because the other hospices nurses didn't expect her to make it. So I held her hand all night and went through all the normal things that you go through when a family member is transitioning, except that at about 5am that morning, I went and laid on the couch in her room and I went to sleep. I woke up because they (the hospice staff) put streamers in her room…they literally had twelve dozen roses from her nurses and colleagues that loved her.

The streamers I thought, were hitting the wall…clap, clap, clap…almost as if a fan was going. And then I heard her say, 'Jeremy if you're going to say goodbye, you need to get up and do it now'. I remember clearly the experience in my mind: in my mind it was like I was a teenager and my mother was waking me up to go to school, or something like that. And I replied (in my mind), 'yea, yea, yea….in a few minutes'.

Right when that happened her secretary knocked on the door and wanted to say goodbye to her, and so woke me up. I too said

'Goodbye' and I lay back down. Around five or ten minutes later, I felt myself lift out of my body - like you're being raised out of the body. What brought me back into the body were the nurses actually tapping me on the shoulder and saying, 'Mr McDonald, you're mum just passed'. And so, I got up and sat there and I said in my mind, 'mum, you're not going to be able to read my book.' And I hear a response in my head, 'Honey, I taught you everything in that book'. This was her voice. She was sitting next to me as if she never left. So, I sat in the room for a while. I brushed my teeth and was going through the whole conversation with her.

A few days later I had another experience. I was in the shower and I felt her spirit step inside of my body and I heard her say, 'this is what heaven feels like and this is what God feels like'. I lost the sensation of my body - it felt like eternity, but in truth it probably lasted about 5-10 seconds. I could tell that the body was there, but I lost all the pain, anxiety, and all the normal mind chatter.

Some people would refer to that as stillness. The best way to describe it is like I was the entire ocean. I felt so overwhelmed and excited because I thought, 'wow, this is the greatest feeling that I have ever experienced in my life, everybody has to experience this', and she told me, 'only when they're ready Jeremy'. And then my mind took me out of it.

My mother wanted to give me a glimpse of what the flow of the universe felt like…what God feels like. It was about God not having any judgement and the cosmos not having any barriers or limitations. She was trying to tell me that although she had experienced death, she was still very much alive. [17]

Out-of-Body Experiences

Whilst an out-of-body experience (OBE) can occur as part of a near-death-experience, it can also occur on its own too. According to the Oxford Dictionary, an OBE is *the sensation of being outsides one's body, typically of floating and being able to observe oneself from a distance.* Mercedes Leal, author of *The Miracle Code – Your Illuminating Bridge to Love Freedom*

Celebration shares her experience:

> *In 1982 I had my first out of body experience. It was 3 o'clock in the morning. I had just glanced at my clock. It was a time when I often awoke, inexplicably. Suddenly, I found myself in a different place. There were no tunnels and there was no light. I was in was my bed one minute and then I was immediately in this other paradise of love, the next. What surprised me in this place was the personality of Nature, because there were trees and grass which welcomed me with more devotional, joyous hospitality than humans, apart from my saintly mother and a few of her ilk.*
>
> *The new tendrils of young leaves on trees reached down playfully to ruffle my hair, like toddlers would, as I glided beneath their shade. I could not see myself but felt the energetic images of my human form. These playful leaves were giggling sweetly and I could hear as well as feel their glee at seeing me. I felt joy too, for them and reached up to ruffle them back, gently and equally lovingly.*
>
> *The trunk was male and paternalistically, sturdily protective of me and the branches and older leaves felt maternally caring. It was if the whole family was interconnected, in one tree and all of the parts loved me dearly and welcomed me as a part of their botanic world. It felt far more homely than the earthly apartment I had left behind. I so wanted to remain. I thought too that I had loved my mother and daughter deeply but in this magnificent Garden of Eden, love was on a whole new level of total, devotional acceptance. I realised instantly that few people would ever know what real love was. It was far, far greater than anything I had ever known and nothing on earth mattered any more.*
>
> *The grass offered the same welcome, as if each blade had known and loved me for aeons. It looked like early twilight, for there was a dimness about the scene, yet I could still see everything clearly, way into to the distance. I saw and felt purest, most peaceful, divine love wherever I looked. There was none of this 'duality' that people speak about: there was just pure, devotional, all accepting, altruistic*

and joyful love and the most heart-warming welcome. I knew this was my home. I so fervently wanted to remain.

Then in the distance, I saw a woman whom I knew instantly, through telepathic connection, was my Mother's sister, but I had never before seen or heard of her and yet instantly, I was sure of her identity. Immediately she realised I wanted to know more about her and was invading her space, she erected an invisible wall between us that told me I had probed too far. I could feel her concern as she told me telepathically that I 'must go back' and that my time was 'not right'.

I looked at my aunt, raised my intent and replied that I was going to stay because I loved my real home. This battling, mental conversation continued for a short while and I could feel her concern rising, as if she feared for me in some way. It was all borne of protection; but she could not stop me from staying. I seemed to over-rule her sweet, gentle ways and it felt so naturally easy; but my comeuppance was close. It was not that she had been weaker than I was but that she was simply more gracious. I was the invading, spiritual barbarian and her true power would soon herald my definite, if loving, dismissal.

I could feel that my aunt was alarmed and agitated by my presence and was telepathically summoning help from a point behind and above me, to my right. She had gone over my head, literally; and although I was looking at her and feeling the enveloping love from the environment around me, I suddenly felt this same high calibre love magnify million-fold where her gaze had focused. I felt it turning into a magical, tangible, brilliant beacon of warmest, twinkling passion, increasing to my right, just behind me, where my aunt was still staring intently. She had manifested something special, it seemed.

As I turned around, unable to contain my curiosity, I could see one massive set of inner, oval glows of light coming towards me, about 20 feet high, intensifying as they went inwards, where the light was brightest; as I looked up to face it, although I could not see eyes, I felt locked visually and emotionally into the love of this being, which was expanding and extending to touch me, enter my soul and take

48

over all my personal space.

I saw in the midst of those giant oval glows, the shape of a brightly illuminated face and human form without features, about eight to ten feet tall on shoulders in a brilliant robe of light that reached to the floor. It was pure, whitest, brightest, highest wattage illumination.

This was the most magnificent, outstanding power that now stood before me. As this being of light looked down on me, I could feel myself absorbing its light until my whole being became brightly illuminated. As my body became a part of the same light, I melted into this figure in front of me, so we became one. I could feel this light in me then being turned up more and more as I grew brighter and brighter in terms of illumination, and a dazzling excitement started to develop, as I was shown all the different types of love that exist: love for one's romantic partner, love for one's parents, love for one's children, love for one's siblings and friends. I was shown all types of love in layers, until they all merged together into one massive, brightly throbbing source of devotional purity and that thrill rose to heightened ecstasy and just kept rising and rising. I thought it would never stop and I loved it. It was extraordinarily, unspeakably thrilling. It was the most exalting experience I had ever known and it's hard to find words to describe it, for none exist which come even close. These primitive words are frustrating.

When that ecstasy rose to the sharpest, most passionate - yet utterly chaste - pinnacle of bliss, suddenly I became aware that I was looking into the face of The Supreme Creator, and with that realisation came the final, explosive burst of brightest, adorational love, light and spiritual empowerment in a flash which seemed to light me up enough to fill the Universe with illuminated adoration. At that high peak of glorious bliss, I was given all the important messages about my life. I was told what I was expected to do. I was told the duties I had to my mother and daughter that I 'had not yet fulfilled' and that I 'MUST go back'. The Being then looked at me with extraordinary tenderness and I saw it showed the brightest, twinkling glow of humour, which was unexpected, and told me that 'whatever' I did, I 'would always be loved'. All my Sunday school teachings dissolved in that moment. I felt liberated from the restrictions of religion. I was freed to fly and to love without boundaries placed by expectation of reciprocity. I knew I would never experience greater love than this.

There was no doubt the being was primarily a paternalistic, deeply accepting and loving energy but yet the adoration for me was as tenderly caring as a mother's. I have never known such love or happiness and with his sweet, final message that I 'must go back', I could feel myself moving backwards. Within a split second, I was once again in my bed. I never saw my aunt again but was very curious about her. If she had existed, it would confirm I had been on a genuine out of body journey and had not merely had a good dream.

The next morning I could not wait to tell my mother about my experience. She listened excitedly, until I reached the part about her sister and then she turned away from me. She refused to discuss or confirm the existence of the aunt I had seen. It was a big blow, but I had to wait a very long time for her response to this life changing experience. In the meantime, my life, jobs and loves got phenomenally better and better and new healing, clairvoyant and telepathic abilities developed naturally, surprising me and those who started to benefit from them. I also started to meet wonderfully magical people.

It was not until ten years later that my Mother invited me one afternoon to sit with her because she thought her life was coming to an end. I was sad but she wanted me to know the truth about that very unusual experience and her Mother's history of shamanism, which no one had ever shared with me. It was a major turning point.

My Mother told me that when she was six years old, her Mother sent her and all her sisters to a catholic convent as boarders. She explained that for the next six years, they had no visits from their parents who lived abroad and neither did they return home. My Mother went on to say that she had a sister two years older than she was, who really took good care of her - almost like a surrogate mother - but that sister became ill at fourteen and died two days later. My heartbroken Mother explained that the pain of her sister's passing was so strong that she never got over the death. She had simply buried it deeply to avoid facing the loss of her favourite sibling.

My Mother then went on to say that the lady I had met and described during my experience was, indeed, her departed sister. She told me that not even my Father knew of that sister's existence, because she hadn't told anyone about her.

Considering that none of us knew about her sibling, this admittance by my Mother confirmed to both me and her that I had not just had a dream but had travelled somewhere very special, beyond human reality. It confirmed life continued beyond 'death'. Later, I applied 'God' as an easy way to help people to understand the experience; but the figure I saw had no name. I just KNEW with absolute certainty, that he - for paternity was the dominant gender I sensed - was the most supremely magical Creator of all that is in my world. I also knew that the highest, vibrational peak of divine adoration, not mere love, is what unites us to his liberating and empowering light and transforms us into his radiant, magnetic and joyful image.

All my Sunday school, religious views dissolved. I saw there was no judgement, no fire, hell and damnation and the Creator is the pinnacle of purest, most miraculous and brilliantly guiding, accepting, joyously devotional, Light.

Now, I can revisit that magical image and place at will. I see life not in terms of ephemeral, human incarnations but as a perpetual continuum of learning, in order to acquire increasing wattage of light through escalating, divine adoration for all that exists. [18]

Mercedes' experience is already a fascinating one - and from an objective point of view, especially because her Mother was able to verify part of it. However, it didn't just end there. Although Mercedes does not wish to reveal what she later went on to tell me, I can say that this experience played an essential role in an event that she experienced years later.

The individuals that I interviewed for this book had remarkable stories for which many would say, there is no logical explanation. In his interview with

Lilou Mace, Dr. Van Lommel made an interesting point. He stated about these phenomena, (NDEs and OBEs):

> *"I never try to convince people ever…at the beginning I was reluctant to believe as well, but over time my scientific curiosity changed and there was an inner knowing that this is the truth. There is only consciousness, and all our physical aspects are just temporary aspects of who we are."* [19]

My own journey too has also brought me to a similar conclusion. I am not here to convince anyone that NDEs and OBEs are real. Through connecting with people who have had near-death and out-of-body experiences, as well as connecting with medical professionals who have come across these cases, I agree that there is an inner knowing that there is truth in these experiences.

One of the reasons that Susan (the client I referred to in the previous chapter), came to see me was because she was finding it very difficult coping with the passing of her mother. Susan said that she was finding it hard because although deep down she still felt her mother's presence at times, the concept of death made her uncomfortable. So, together in sessions we started to explore aspects of the Transcendent Mind and I shared with Susan some of the case studies that I had come across, as well as some of the research that has been done in this field. Susan commented that this process had really helped her because it also tied in with her religious faith, as she believed that Human Beings were on a journey to become one with their Creator, to become whole once again.

Although unsure about death, there was a part of Susan that believed that an aspect of us moved on once we die, but this wasn't a conversation that she often had with people. Studying aspects of the Transcendent Mind had introduced Susan to research and case studies that she had never really considered before, and through doing so she had found a sense of peace, an inner knowing that somehow we were all connected and that forgiveness and compassion is what we needed to work on.

Another one of my male clients who had just turned 25 came to see me because he was suffering from anxiety. During the sessions, it transpired that he had had a fear of death, as through the years he had lost a few family members and friends. He had grown up in a family where it was believed that death marked the end of an individual's existence and that nothing further existed. Although he didn't judge his family in any way, he said that there was a part of him that just couldn't come to terms with the fact that dying was the end. He realised that the anxiety was the result of him not being able to express his thoughts and feelings with anyone. This, for him, was a delicate topic and he was afraid of upsetting those around him. However, once he started to explore other viewpoints on death and dying, his anxiety disappeared.

Regardless of their age, sex or culture, there have been people from all over the world who have reported having had either near-death or out-of-body experiences - with many of these individuals experiencing the core elements that Dr. Raymond Moody mentions in his books[7]. Although some individuals will continue to look for an alternative explanation, we cannot ignore some of the miraculous occurrences that have taken place.

It has also been reported that individuals who have an NDE, experience both psychological and physiological changes. For example, according to P.M.H Atwater, around 80% of individuals who experience NDEs change as a result. They experience factors such as becoming more spiritual than religious, no longer being afraid of death and, developing a sense of timelessness. [20]

These individuals recognise a deeper truth and are able to remember directly their experience of the infinite Transcendent Mind. Most of them no longer need external verification, as their subjective experience stands strong within. However, for those of us who have not experienced an NDE or OBE, considering the possibility of an infinite, omnipresent Transcendent Mind may lead to deeper emotional healing. Questioning both who we really are at the very core, and our purpose in the grander scheme of things, may well be what is required for us to lead more of a peaceful, compassionate, forgiving life.

---

7   If you would like to learn more about Dr. Raymond Moody and his work, please visit www. lifeafterlife.com

3
The Interconnected Transcendent Mind

"All differences in this world are of degree, and not of kind,
because oneness is the secret of everything."
- Swami Vivekananda

In 1971, Apollo 14 Astronaut Edgar Mitchell experienced an epiphany whilst travelling back to Earth from the Moon. Watching the Earth from the window seat, he experienced a profound sense of interconnectedness:

"We were rotating every two minutes to keep thermo balance on the spacecraft, so what that allowed to have happened, was that every two minutes I saw the Earth, the Sun and the Moon and a 360 degree panorama of the heavens, like I had never seen before. The magnificence of seeing this, particularly since it was from space, is that the Heavens are ten times as bright, starts ten times as numerous than you can ever see from the surface of the Earth because of the intervening atmosphere. But what this triggered in my visioning was the fact that the magnificence of all of this, and the understanding from my studies of astronomy at Harvard and MIT during my Doctoral work, was the understanding that all matter in our Universe is created in star systems. And so the matter in my body, the matter in my spacecraft, the matter in my partners' bodies was the product of stars and we can consider that stardust – we are stardust, and we're all one in that sense. And I did not understand the origin of that

experience – why or how it happened. And it continued for three days coming home." [1]

When Edgar Mitchell returned home, he looked through scientific and religious literature to try and make sense of his experience, however he couldn't find an explanation. He later learned from a group of anthropologists and archaeologists from a nearby University, that experiences similar to his had been documented in ancient Sanskrit as *Samadhi* - which meant that although things are seen through the senses as they are, they are experienced viscerally and internally as a unity and a oneness, accompanied by a feeling of ecstasy. In his interview, Edgar Mitchell also went on to say that the Greeks referred to this experience as *Metanoria,* meaning a change of mind or heart; and the Zen Buddhists call it *Satori,* which means sudden enlightenment.

As this chapter is all about the interconnected aspect of the Transcendent Mind, let's explore for a moment what the term *interconnected* means in this context. In the example above, Edgar Mitchell experienced a sense of oneness – that everything was interconnected in some way. In fact his experience sounds very much like Maslow's definition of a *peak experience,* (which was regarded as a mystical illumination or revelation). But, interconnectedness isn't just this feeling of oneness that many individuals experience.

Let's revisit the definition of the Transcendent Mind: it is *a Mind that not only goes beyond our individual minds, but also includes our personal, individualised minds too. It is common to us all and is responsible for the experience of interconnectedness. The Transcendent Mind is an all-pervading consciousness that has the ability to transcend time and space.* Therefore, if we all share and are part of a Transcendent Mind, then interconnectedness can be observed and experienced in a number of ways which include not only the sense of oneness, but also precognition, sixth sense and telepathy (both with humans and other sentient beings such as animals and plants).

The existence of a Transcendent Mind would also help to explain the rapid, unexplainable healing that some individuals experience – a type of healing that cannot be explained in a logical sense. This is the type of healing that seems to transcend time, for example, in the case of Anita Moorjani (chapter two), who experienced the rapid healing of her cancer after her near-death experience.

Cristina from Brazil says that she has experienced precognition and other forms of extra-sensory perception since childhood. In the following passage, Cristina talks about a precognitive dream that she experienced a few years ago:

"It's almost always related to dreams for me. This is how I receive information. There was one experience that I had when I was sleeping a while back. I'll call it a dream, but it wasn't really a regular dream. I can't find the words to describe exactly what the experience was like - it was very different. It was almost as if I was out of my body and I could feel that there were spirits by my side. Anyway, in this state I saw in my room a very big movie screen and I was watching it. There was a famous actress from Brazil on this screen and a guy came over to her on this screen and he killed her. Whilst still in this dream state, I can remember saying 'NO! You can't do this.' I realised that the actress and the man that I could see on this screen had been involved in a secret romance and this is why the murder had happened.

The next morning I told my husband about the dream that I had had. Shortly afterwards I learned from a newspaper that the actress had been killed by that man in exactly the same way that I had seen in my dream. It was years later that people finally discovered that the actress and the man that had murdered her had been involved in a secret romance." [2]

Cristina has also experienced receiving other messages through dreams:

"On one occasion my ex-sister-in-law wasn't feeling too well. She was experiencing some emotional problems and she was really going through a difficult experiences. At the time, I was taking medicinal herb classes and so she asked me whether I could recommend any herbs that may be able to help her. So I had started to research herbs

based on what she had told me, but despite researching for much of the day, I couldn't find anything and so I went to bed without any answers.

During the night I had a dream in which a herb was shown to me. This particular herb is well known for its healing properties, most specifically to do with ulcers. When I woke up in the morning and reflected on the dream, I thought it was odd that this particular herb had come up because it didn't have the healing properties that matched her symptoms. I called her that morning anyway to see how she was, and it was then that told me that she had just been to the doctors and had been diagnosed with a stomach ulcer - a symptom that the herb I dreamt about could be used to treat." [3]

Dr. Cleve Backster & Biocommunication

So far in this chapter we have looked at personal experiences and messages from a few spiritual texts. In this section we will now explore the work of Dr. Cleve Backster, whose fascinating findings suggest that our thoughts interact with our environment.

Dr. Cleve Backster became fascinated with hypnosis in his teens when he was a student attending Rutgers Prep School - a boarding school which was then part of Rutgers University in New Jersey. Backster soon learned (after several successful experiences) that hypnosis was a powerful process, and continued to work with hypnosis in the years to come. After working for the U.S Navy and the U.S Army Counter-Intelligence Corps, Backster went on to work for the CIA. It was during this time that he received training from Leonarde Peeler who was a pioneer in the use of the polygraph - which is also known as a lie detector. A few years later Backster went on to establish his own commercial polygraph consultant business, and in 1959 moved to New York City. [4]

Although he had an interest in hypnosis, Backster had never really thought about becoming involved in consciousness research. However on February 2nd 1966, Backster made a paradigm-changing discovery:

"On February 2, 1966, an event occurred that expanded the entire focus of my research through a kind of paradigm shift in my own

awareness. At the time I had been involved for 18 years in the use of polygraph testing on humans. I was taking an early morning coffee break and decided to water the dracaena cane plant that my secretary had brought into the laboratory. After pouring water into the pot of soil at its base, I wondered if I could measure the rate of moisture as it ascended. I attached the end of a large leaf to the galvanic-skin-response section of the polygraph instrument. The plant leaf was successfully balanced into the polygraph's Wheatstone bridge circuitry, which I planned to use as a means of reflecting the rate of moisture ascent. The relative increase in the leaf's electrical conductivity—due to the expected change in its moisture content—would be indicated by an upward trending of the ink tracing on the chart recording. To my surprise, the plant leaf tracing initially exhibited a downward trending, which would ordinarily indicate increasing resistance. Then, about one minute into the chart recording, the tracing exhibited a contour similar to the reaction pattern of a human subject attached to a polygraph who might have been briefly experiencing the fear of detection. I thought: Well, if this plant wants to show me some people-like reactions, I've got to use some people-like rules on it and see if I can get this to happen again. "I decided to figure out how I could threaten the well-being of the plant. I wasn't into talking to plants— not at that time—so as a substitute threat I immersed the end of a leaf, which was neighboring the electrode leaf, into a cup of hot coffee. There was no noticeable chart reaction, and there was a continuing downward-tracing trend. With a human, this downward trend would indicate fatigue or boredom. Then, after about 15 minutes of elapsed chart time, I had this thought: As the ultimate plant threat, I would get a match and burn its electrode leaf. At that time, the plant was about 15 feet away and the polygraph equipment was about 5 feet away from where I was standing. It was early in the morning and no other person was in the laboratory. At that moment my thought and intent was 'I'm gonna burn that leaf!' just to see what the plant would do. The second the imagery of burning the leaf entered my mind, the recording pen jumped to the top of the chart! No words were spoken, no touching the plant, no lighting of matches, just the clear intention to burn the leaf. The plant recording showed wild excitation. To me, this was a powerful, high-quality observation."[5]

As Backster continued his experiments, he made some interesting discoveries. He found that emotions played a substantial part in conducting the polygraph test. For example, in order to observe a chart reaction there had to be real intent to harm the plant. It was as if the plant knew the difference between someone expressing a real intent of harm or someone merely pretending to want to harm the plant.[6]

Another interesting observation that Backster made was that plants became attuned to their territory. For example, they could sense information sixty or seventy feet away within their attuned area, but yet they weren't able to sense information from a space twenty feet away to which they were not attuned, such as a the unconnected lab next door. [7]. In addition to this, the plants also appeared to form a bond with their caretakers. On occasion when Backster had been out running errands and had made a spontaneous decision to return back to the lab, he found the chart reading showed that the plant had a significant reaction at that time. The mere thought of going back would not produce the same result, as the significant reaction would only occur if Backster actually made the decision to return to the lab. What is interesting about this is that how the plant is attuned to the individual even once the individual is in a remote location. It would appear that as long as the plant is attuned to the individual, distance is not an issue. Backster describes another example: [8].

"Once during this early phase of plant observation my associate, Bob Henson, was about to experience a wedding anniversary and his wife Mary-Ann, wanted my collaboration for a surprise party in Clifton, New Jersey. He was a Scorpio and I had been told that it's difficult to hide things from them, so I figured out how to pull this off: I'd get him to collaborate on another plant experiment involving possible lab plant changes as he and I made the trip from New York City to Clifton. The electrode plant should be attuned to both Bob and myself. On this occasion we kept careful research notes as our trip to Clifton progressed. Aside from accomplishing the original surprise party

mission, it turned out to be a rather successful experiment. Later that night when I returned to the lab to compare the pant response times with the notes we had taken, there were noticeable changes in the reaction patterns at various stages of our trip: When we walked the underground approach from Times Square to Port Authority Terminal at 40th Street and Eight Avenue; when we boarded the bus for Clifton; when the bus entered the Lincoln Tunnel travelling from Manhattan to New Jersey, and during the remaining trip to Clifton. Mary Ann had set the party preparations at a neighbour's house in Clifton so as to keep the secret, and it worked. As we approached the house, everyone yelled, "Surprise! Happy Anniversary!" Upon checking the chart recording back in the New York City lab, there was a big reaction from the plant at that exact time." [9]

Backster discovered that plants were also attuned to the death of other microscopic life forms. For example, the plants would respond intensely when hot water was poured down the sink and hit the drain. In this instance it was later confirmed that there was bacteria present in the drain of the sink, which according to Backster appeared to be emitting some type of signal when the water was poured down the sink - hence enabling the plant to perceive some form of a threat. [10]

If you want to learn more about Cleve Backster's work, then I would suggest you read his book *Primary Perception,* in which Backster goes on to discuss other research findings with eggs, yogurt bacteria and even with live human cells. This research suggests that all living entities are connected or attuned to their environment. He also discusses his attempts to follow scientific methodology for his research[8], and the fact that he believed that the biocommunication that was taking place was *not* within any form of signal that could be shielded by ordinary means, such as electromagnetic frequencies. [11]

---

8   Backster's research was published in 1968 in the International Journal of Parapsychology.

Other Findings

There have been a number of studies published in recent years that suggest that parapsychological phenomena, such as telepathy, clairvoyance and psychokinesis (mind over matter) may exist. Let's take a look at a handful of the findings.

In a study conducted in 1994 by Grinberg-Zylberbaum et al, it was found that (with appropriate interaction), it is possible for the human brain to establish close relationships with another brain. This study demonstrated non-locality of brain responses in the following way: pairs of subjects were allowed to interact and then were placed in individual Faraday cages, where their EEG activity was registered. Then, one of the subjects from each pair was shown a series of light flashes. Now here's the interesting part: the subject that was shown the flashes naturally displayed brain activity that was recorded by the EEG machine, but the non-stimulated subject also showed "transferred potentials" similar to those evoked in the stimulated subject. [12]

In 2001, a paper published in BMJ reported the results of an investigation that looked at the effects of remote, retroactive intercessory prayer on outcomes in patients with bloodstream infection. It was found that the prayer was associated with both a shorter duration of fever in patients, as well as a shorter stay in hospital. The paper concluded that remote, retroactive, intercessory prayer should be considered for use in clinical practice. [13]

In a study that was published in 2004, Radin et al. sought to explore the effects of healing intention and intentional space conditioning on the growth of cultured human brain cells and the distribution of truly random events. The study found a single application of healing intention may not be enough to affect human brain cell colony formation or random number generators to a significant degree. However, repeated application of space conditioning and healing intention meditations appear to have measurable consequences in both systems. [14]

In 2008, Explore published a study conducted by Radin et al. which concluded that directing intention towards a distant person is associated with activation of that person's autonomic nervous system.

In other words, one's nervous system seems to be affected simply when another person directs at tention towards them. This is an interesting finding as it points towards the power of our intentions and our ability to affect another. The study also concluded that strong motivation to both heal and be healed, as well as training on how to develop and direct compassionate intention may enhance this effect further. [15]

As well as for my own interest and as part of research for this book, I undertook a short course in Parapsychology with The University of Edinburgh in the latter part of 2013. During this time I was exposed to many parapsychological studies and views of both proponents and sceptics. What I came to understand was that there have been many studies conducted which suggest the existence of parapsychological phenomena (psi), and then there are the sceptics who challenge research findings and suggest alternative explanations for results. For example, it has been suggested that there are psychological explanations for some of the findings and also that some findings have come about due to fraud. Personally I feel that perhaps these may be plausible explanations in some cases, but that does not mean that genuine parapsychological psi does not exist either.

Looking at the studies that have been conducted within the last century, I don't think that we can deny the existence of psi. There have been numerous, good quality studies that suggest that psi is a genuine phenomena, and that what needs to now be explored are theoretical explanations and improvements in methodology.

You may be wondering why this evidence is not talked about more, or even taught widely at university? This is one of the first things that I wondered too. When I first became interested in studying this topic further, I turned to universities thinking that they would be an avenue for me to explore more about this subject. However, I was surprised to find that although some institutions taught modules, not many of them provided an in depth study option. My area of interest was near-death studies but after speaking to some lecturers at different universities I realised that it was going to be a challenge finding supervision for PhD study.

Although psi phenomena appears to be more accepted in the eastern world, it is still not taken as seriously in western society. I believe there are a number of reasons as to why people don't take psi phenomena seriously. Let's take a look:

Preconceived ideas about psi

Paranormal phenomena is something that is widely known about in society, but is not necessarily a topic that the general public is accurately informed about. We form preconceived ideas about psi from a number of sources including movies, media, religion and upbringing.

I believe that our preconceived ideas may create a bias within us (sometimes even without us realising), and this then influences our judgement about a particular topic. The fact of the matter is that we are not machines. We are all human and we all experience emotions and feelings, hence it becomes very difficult for many of us to stay objective about a topic - as sometimes we cannot help but form judgments. I have spoken to some people who have such a strong belief that psi phenomena is not real, that they are not even willing to consider the research. Their preconceived views have influenced their ability to remain open-minded.

Psi challenges our current scientific model

I studied a degree in maths, science and education and then went on to become a teacher. Although I had somewhat of an interest in my chosen career path, I couldn't imagine teaching in educational institutions for the rest of my life. However, on the other hand I didn't know what else I wanted to do. It took me a while to discover that the link between science, spirituality and emotional healing was my calling - and even that I stumbled upon by accident when I became interested in hypnotherapy.

In time I realised that the reason it took me so long to discover and manifest my inner calling, was because I wasn't exposed to this area of research whilst I was growing up. There was some part of me that knew that I was here to do something specific, only I didn't know what it was. I would occasionally come across reports in the media that talked about the power of the mind or near death experiences and I would find these fascinating, but it wasn't really something that I felt I could speak to my teachers, lecturers or peers about because it wasn't 'scientific enough'. I found that many of my peers didn't take this topic seriously and considered it to be 'woo-woo'. They couldn't see the significance of investigating it further - especially because it couldn't be explained by the widely accepted scientific model – the Newtonian world view.

I believe that Newtonian science has made some phenomenal advances over the years in areas such as medicine and space travel. However, in my opinion science has also become somewhat arrogant and closed-minded. In a latter part of the 19th century a young man in Germany who was considering a career in physics was advised against it. He was told that there was nothing much left to discover in this field and that he should consider an alternative path. This young man's name was Max Planck – who today is often referred to as *founding father of the quantum.*

Einstein was right when he said, *"The most beautiful thing we can experience is the mysterious. It is the source of all true art and all science. He to whom this emotion is a stranger, who can no longer pause to wonder and stand rapt in awe, is as good as dead: his eyes are closed."* [16] When we start believing that we have most of the answers about the environment in which we live, we cut off our curiosity. We have arrived here today by building upon the ideas that our ancestors put forward. No one person has explained everything themselves, but rather different people have made different contributions throughout time and this is how we have advanced in knowledge.

We have been educated in institutions that give predominance to classical physics – the Newtonian model. Psi challenges this because it presents phenomena that cannot be explained by Newtonian science. This means that we have to alter our perception both about science and the world in which we live. This can be unsettling for us because we then have to admit that although we have made some great progress, we do not yet understand everything about our environment or about the way in which things function. In Cleve Backster's book, Primary Perception he shares some of the responses that he had in relation to his work. Yale Professor, Arthur Galston commented:

"This is a field of work which attracts quacks, charlatans and people who lack professional credentials. It's not a field into which many reputable workers have cared to venture. I don't say Backster's

phenomena are impossible. I just say there are enough other things of more value to work on. It's attractive to think that plants are listening to you or they respond to prayer, but there's nothing in it. There's no nervous system in a plant. There are no means by which sensation can be transferred." [17]

Whilst I agree that there are other things of value to work on too, I also believe that Backster's research is profound. What could be more important than learning about who we are and how we interact with the environment? Addressing this question will not only help enhance our experience of life, but will also help guide our future generations. Just because our current scientific model cannot explain some of these findings does not mean that they do not exist. Perhaps it is time that we expand our current view of science and look for ways that can explain these occurrences. Yes, it is likely that there are some charlatans out there and that some of the findings may have been the result of fraud. It is also likely that in some cases, psychology may provide valid explanations for some of the unexplainable occurrences. However, this does not mean that all psi phenomena are not genuine.

Rather than approaching the topic from the black-and-white perspective of whether psi is real or not, I believe we need to carefully consider the findings with an open mind. The truth of the matter is that as long as we have good quality experiments that suggest the existence of psi, it still remains an area that needs further research and study - especially because the implications of understanding these phenomena could be profound for mankind.

Cultural differences

Cultural differences between eastern and western societies also play a part. For example, in eastern cultures concepts such as the existence of a higher power and the soul moving on after the death of the physical body are widely accepted notions. Faith rituals, prayer and ceremonies also play an important part in these traditions and are frequently used to try and enhance the quality of one's life. Furthermore, paranormal activity is generally accepted as a real phenomenon and appropriate steps are taken to ensure that souls pass over comfortably after death. Remember the case study that I shared in chapter two about J's uncle unable to pass on properly after death? Well, it is likely that many more such case studies exist. There is an understanding amongst eastern traditions that although we appear to separate beings, we are also connected at a very deep level. There is the belief that we all come from the one Source.

If we're talking labels, then I would be labelled as a British Asian, and you could say faith has been an integral part of my upbringing. One of the things that I have found to be fascinating, is watching some of my family members establish successful scientific careers for themselves and yet still maintain a strong faith in a higher power. These individuals regard science and faith to be different manifestations of one life. In other words, they believe that one higher power is the source of everything. The findings of psi research come as no great surprise to these people.

Growing up I discovered that (interestingly) not everyone holds this viewpoint. I learned that some of the western world had a different view, where individuals were viewed as separate units completely. There was a heavy focus on the mind and intellect, with faith and science being regarded as two separate areas. I believe this is one of the reasons that we do not commonly come across psi research. If an individual has a mechanistic worldview, it is a possibility that they may not consider psi research to be of much significance and hence not a common topic of discussion.

Daunting on a personal level

Accepting the existence of psi phenomena may be daunting on a personal level for some individuals. If we have grown up believing that psi doesn't exist and is something that is only found in the fantasy world of books, then it may be unsettling for us to consider an alternative view. For example, death is one such area that is sensitive topic for many people. Believing that there is nothing after death, and then learning that there may be a possibility of 'life after death' can be an unsettling thought as for some it will shake the very foundation of their belief system, prompting them to reconsider who they really are.

A New Scientific Worldview

In January 2013 I conducted an interview with Chief Scientist of the Institute of Noetic Sciences Dr Radin states:

"I've always been interested in things that don't fit. If you look at our current mainstream way of thinking of consciousness, it is regarded as something arising from the brain. The brain is a complex object and there are lots of recursive loops and maybe it is this self-reflection that is happening in the brain's structure that gives rise to consciousness. There is some evidence that looks like it may be correct. But there are also anomalies that people talk about which sounds like it's not part of the brain, and here I am talking about things like clairvoyance - where somehow people are able to get information from a far distance without the use of ordinary senses; or precognition or telepathy or any of the psychic phenomena. They don't seem to fit into the brain based models of consciousness. So, I focussed on these anomalies because it's always the anomalies that show where your assumptions break down in current theories. If you understand the anomalies better, then the likelihood is that you would be able to make a much greater advancement in your understanding. That is why I focus on psychic phenomena.

Over the past twenty years or so I've looked at each of the major categories of psychic phenomena. I would say that we can say with high certainty that phenomena like telepathy, clairvoyance, precognition and some forms of mind-matter interaction exist because of scientific evidence. Of course when I say that, what comes to people's minds is that every T.V show, movie and novel that they have ever read like Harry Potter is true? Well no, those are embellishments. But the basic idea that these phenomena exist is as close to being as certain as science is able to have anything.

The nature of the evidence now and has always been statistical but that's not too surprising because the nature of anything we know about psychological factors is also statistical. People are highly variable so we do lots of experiments. It takes a lot of repeated trials in order to reach a conclusion. We have very high confidence that these phenomena exist. The importance of this is that the anomalies are still anomalous, even though we know that they exist. The anomalies are useful because it tells us that when we try to create a model of what we think consciousness is, where it comes from and its capacities, we have to include psychic phenomena in that model otherwise it is incomplete." [18]

Dr. Radin has raised an important point about anomalies: that if studied in more detail they may help to expand our current views and theories. My main aim for researching and writing this book was to find out more about who we really are as human beings, what makes us conscious and how does this impact our emotional wellbeing? If you remember, my main issue was how could we heal ourselves emotionally if we don't understand who we really are? Rather than attempting to answer this question from one perspective, (for example just psychology), I believed that we needed to take a multi-disciplinary approach. We need to look at findings for different disciplines, consider different schools of thought and see whether there is a common thread that runs throughout them. The issue with looking at just one perspective is that we don't always get to see the bigger picture. If we tried to understand the nature of our being and existence solely through religion, there's a good chance that we would only uncover part of the story as there are some limitations that we would have to consider. For example, we cannot be certain that the religious texts that we refer to contain the original message that was intended. Neither do we know how the text has changed throughout the ages or even if they have been interpreted correctly through translation.

We can however expand our view and instead of looking at the differences between different religions, begin to look for similarities. We can look to science, psychology, parapsychology and neuroscience to see whether any explanations can be found. In this way we gain a wider and more realistic understanding of what we're dealing with. Rather than looking at science and God as two different areas, we can begin to use science to redefine our perception of God.

After looking at parapsychological studies and doing lots of research on near-death and-out-of-body experiences, I was curious to discover what science had to say about these findings and also, about whom we really are. Was there a scientific explanation to be found? And if so, why are we not aware it?

Prior to the last quarter of the 19th century, it was thought that there was nothing much new to discover in physics. Physics was centred on Newton's laws and Maxwell's electromagnetism, and any ideas that contradicted this classical viewpoint would not be given much consideration. Classical physicists believed that the Universe was mechanistic in nature and operated within the framework of time and space. Furthermore, Newton's equations could be used to predict the future, or even gain knowledge about the past if enough was known about particles at a given point in time.

There is no space for a Transcendent Mind in this model of physics because it is thought that everything is made up of particles of matter. In other words, the particles make up atoms, which make up molecules, which then make up cells. It is thought that the brain is made up in this way and that consciousness arises from the brain. There is no explanation for phenomena such as precognition, telepathy or clairvoyance as these suggest that there has to be more at play than just individual human beings that are made up of elementary particles.

Enter quantum physics. In the latter part of the 19th century, gaps in the classical model were apparent and a new branch of physics was taking shape – quantum physics. Quantum physics is the study of matter and energy at the atomic and subatomic levels. (In other words, it is the study of very small things). Quantum physics has helped bring about inventions such as the laser, silicon chips, microwaves and CDs. It is also used to calculate probabilities of possibilities that may occur. Now, these aspects of quantum physics are readily acceptable.

But. Things become strange when we begin to consider *the measurement problem* (also known as *the observer effect)*. The measurement problem poses that an atom only exists in a particular place if it is measured. So, in other words the atom is everywhere, existing as all probabilities until it is consciously observed. This is a profound phenomenon because it suggests that human consciousness may be affecting the environment around us.

In a study that was published in 1997, Schlitz and Wiseman sought to explore experimenter effects [9] and remote detection of staring. (This is the feeling of being stared at, only to turn around and discover that someone is in

---

9   The "experimenter effect" is where the experimenter consciously or unconsciously influences the outcome of an experiment

fact directly looking at you.) In this experiment, there were two types of participants: the "sender" and the "receiver". The aim of the study was to see whether the receivers could psychically detect the gaze directed at them by unseen senders.

The interesting thing about this study is that both authors had previously attempted the study independently. Wiseman is a psi sceptic and failed to find any significant effects. Schlitz on the other hand, is a psi proponent whose study produced positive results. Hence, the authors agreed to do a joint study in order to ascertain why their original independent studies produced such dramatically different results.

The results of the combined study indicated that Schlitz had once again obtained positive results, whereas Wiseman's results were not significant. Limitations were considered carefully in this study, and one of the possible explanations given was that the experimenters could have used their own psi abilities to produce the desired outcomes. However, in conclusion it was stated that this study was the first step to learning more about the experimenter effect in psi research. Further collaboration between sceptics and proponents was suggested. [19] Once again this is a very important area of study because it questions how objective experimentation really is, and whether the observer effect may be at play.

Theoretical Quantum Physicist Dr. Amit Goswami is the pioneer of the new paradigm called *Science within Consciousness*. Goswami states that a revolution in science took place at the beginning of the 20th century when discoveries in quantum physics were made, and that these discoveries support the existence of a God – although perhaps not in the traditional sense.

Goswami asks us to consider consciousness from a different perspective – that rather than look at consciousness as being an epiphenomenon of the brain, which is a materialist perspective; consider instead that consciousness is the *ground of all being*. In other words, everything stems from consciousness. He refers to quantum signatures of the divine as being: *non-locality, discontinuity and tangled hierarchy,* and uses these concepts to explain the existence of psi phenomena as well as the manifestation of miracles. [20]

Clearly, there is a paradigm shift taking place within science too, as there seems to be evidence for a Transcendent Mind emerging. No longer is this a "woolly" concept, but rather an exciting field of study that has the potential to transform humanity. Let's now take a look at how the Transcendent Mind impacts our emotional wellbeing.

Part Two

Transcendent Therapy Healing

4

The Transcendent Healing Process

An Overview

The main reason that I decided to write this book was to introduce you to some of the research in this area and discuss its potential impact on humanity. I believe that if we wish to understand more about ourselves emotionally then we need to be open to the idea that something beyond just our human form exists. As mentioned in an earlier chapter, my interest in this area grew when I questioned why traditional psychotherapy techniques didn't work for everyone. Could it be that we weren't just human bodies and biochemical reactions? And what about individuals that had experienced sudden enlightenment – how had their perception changed so drastically in an instant? As therapy is all about helping people to shift perceptions, I would say that these are very important questions to be asking.

So far this book has highlighted some of the research that indicates the existence of a Transcendent Mind. We learned in the last chapter that after two decades of carrying out consciousness research, Dr. Radin feels that there is a high certainty that psi phenomenon exists.

For me however, the notion of a Transcendent Mind did not come solely as a result of studying research. Whilst the research has been very informative, the findings do not come as a surprise as there has always been a part of me that has felt that there is more to us than meets the eye. Before I turned to parapsychology and science to find answers, I first explored the various faiths. Rather than focussing on the differences between these faiths, I focussed on the similarities and questioned whether there were any common ideas that were prevalent. I found that the concepts of God, love, kindness, empathy, forgiveness and compassion were themes that were present amongst the various faiths. I also realised that just because somebody claims to be 'religious', does not necessarily mean that they are incorporating these aspects into their life. Furthermore, I recognised that these were the very themes that people needed to work on in order to achieve emotional wellbeing. From a practical perspective as a Therapist, I wanted to know *why* these aspects were so important and *why* some individuals were finding it difficult to incorporate them.

And hence the journey of exploration began. For me personally, the concept of a Transcendent Mind evolved from piecing together findings from different disciplines and considering the picture as a whole. But the question then became, 'what relevance did the Transcendent Mind have for us? So there is a high likelihood that we may be able to communicate telepathically and that we may be interconnected in someway, but how did this affect our emotional healing?' Well after a while, it eventually started to make sense.

Emotional healing involves changing our perspective about certain experiences that we have had, and tools such as forgiveness, compassion and empathy are important aspects of the journey. When we recognise that we are part of a greater whole (the Transcendent Mind), forgiveness takes on a whole different meaning. Over the years I have made an interesting observation in that many of us unconditionally forgive our immediate families when they make a mistake. In the past I have heard people say that it doesn't matter how bad an argument you have had with your siblings or your parents, eventually you go 'back to normal' with them. It is as if we have a built-in mechanism that allows us to forgive them with more ease and move on - perhaps it is because we share the same DNA? However, we're not always as forgiving of others to whom we are not related, and we can tend to hold grudges and find it difficult to move on when we feel that we have been wrong done by.

When we recognise who we are and that we're connected at the very core, we open up the doors to changing our perspective on challenging circumstances. We start to view forgiveness with different eyes. To understand this further we need to learn more about how we function.

What is Emotional Wounding?

Emotional wounding is a term that I use to describe the emotional trauma and pain that we experience and internalise over the years. Trauma comes in many different forms and sometimes the briefest of comments can have the deepest effect on us. Barry, a seemingly confident individual, told me that the one factor that had the most impact on him was when his wife discovered that he was having an affair, and told him that he had ruined her life. Barry knew that the affair was very painful for his wife and he had never intended to hurt her. He knew that their relationship had been in trouble for sometime and when the opportunity for the affair arose he found himself 'just going with it'. He was confused about both relationships and when his wife made the discovery and expressed her pain and anger, Barry found it difficult to forgive himself.

In this instance both individuals experienced emotional wounding. Understandably, on making the discovery Barry's wife was both shocked and angry. She commented that she couldn't understand what had happened and would never dream of taking such an action that would hurt her husband so much. She was grief –stricken and didn't know how to process the pain.

Barry on the other hand, said that he had been battling his inner demons for sometime and knew that his wife was a nice person. He also knew that there was no excuse for his behaviour and that he should have addressed their failing relationship through better communication. As a result of the discovery Barry had lost all self-respect for himself, and was left feeling very confused.

There is always a reason behind our actions and part of the healing process is to ask ourselves *why* we behave in certain ways. Questioning our behaviour opens the door to a greater level of self-awareness and helps us to understand the reasoning behind our actions. If we do not have a way of dealing with the pain and trauma that we experience during the years, then these experiences may heavily influence our current behaviour.

Barry hardly ever received any praise whilst he was growing up. Not knowing any better, his parents would criticise his efforts in hope that he would better himself. School wasn't overly a pleasant experience either. Barry's only real passion was Geography and he often found the other subjects boring and hence found it hard to apply himself properly. All of these experiences created emotional wounding and shaped the beliefs that Barry held about himself. Unable to deal with the lack of self-worth that he was developing, Barry turned to other means to seek approval and fill that hole of unworthiness.

As Barry's marriage started to collapse, it triggered off the old emotional wounding and feelings of failure. Barry had never learned how to address these feelings directly, so the only way that he could take the pain away was to entertain another relationship which did not come with any baggage. This relationship was new, fresh and exciting, and at the current stage both individuals had not yet encountered one another's emotionally wounded behaviour. This is because when we first enter a new relationship the focus is quite often on all the positive points. We make an effort for one another: good clothing, good aftershave or perfume and of course…good behaviour. In time however, we encounter obstacles in life that bring to surface our old emotional wounds which cause us to behave in certain ways. A new relationship does not change the unhealed aspects within us; it simply provides an avenue for us to mask them for a while. The only way that we can change our behaviour is to take an honest look at ourselves and work on the healing our wounded hearts.

Underneath the emotionally wounded behaviour, Barry was a good person. Once he understood the reasoning behind his behaviour, he realised it was likely that it would replay out in any relationship. Yes, both him and his wife had to work on their marriage, but more importantly he had to work on himself and he had to address all his false beliefs that he had learned about himself. He had to learn how to face up and deal with his pain rather than finding escape routes that would provide him with only momentary relief.

A vast majority of the world's population is emotionally wounded in some way or another. We grow up in an environment which tells us that we have to be a certain way in order to be accepted, but the truth of the matter is that we all have inner conflicts and we're all human. The aim is not to hide our emotionally wounded aspects, but rather to bring them to the surface and work on healing them. When we are able to accept our own flaws and show ourselves compassion, we are more likely to be more understanding of others too. We will taker a deeper look into emotional wounding in the next chapter.

Time is the Greatest Healer

Over the years I have discovered that there is a natural healing that is taking place within us all the time. This is one of the reasons as to why we tend to become wiser as we get older. In many cases I have seen that even when we do not actively work on our own healing, the pain tends to lessen over time, hence we have the popular saying, 'time is the greatest healer'.

Of course there are cases where people have endured severe emotional trauma and have not been able to process the emotional pain that they have suffered. Hence they remain stuck in the past. They are unable to move past the trauma and even-though years may have passed since the event, they still re-live it on a frequent basis.

The next few chapters are all about the Transcendent Healing Process. Deep healing occurs when we address both our individual natures as well as our transcendent natures. The healing is a combination of understanding more about who we are and how we function; taking responsibility for our thoughts and actions and knowing when to let go of, and surrender a situation. This process also addresses healing from a mind, body and spirit perspective. The following four chapters will cover the healing process in more detail. You will be introduced to a combination of knowledge and techniques that you can apply in order to begin the Transcendent Healing Process. Here is a breakdown of the four elements that make up the Transcendent Healing Process:

Element 1: Understand what emotional wounding is and how it occurs.

The first element involves recognising what emotional wounding is and how it develops with in us. Although I have briefly discussed emotional wounding, this element will explain it in more detail. Here, there are two aspects that we need to become aware of: firstly, how our individual minds function; and secondly the role that the Transcendent Mind plays, and the dichotomies that are created within us. We need to become familiar with our paradoxical nature. The more we understand about ourselves, the better chance we stand of healing ourselves.

The first step is always the intellectual understanding of a concept. Although this is an important part of healing, we must be mindful to incorporate what we have learned into our daily lives. There are many individuals that have the knowledge but fail to apply it, and this is a dangerous place to be because it stunts our personal growth. Real change happens when we move from a place of *knowing* to a place of *doing* and eventually we enter into a state of conscious *being*. This is how change occurs.

Element 2: Understand what emotional healing is and how it occurs.

Once we understand emotional wounding we then need to turn our attention to emotional healing, which is the second element. There is a four-phase process that facilitates emotional healing. This step incorporates both the individual and the Transcendent Mind. In this element we learn more about the role of the Transcendent Mind in the healing process, and how we can activate a deeper healing within ourselves. Understanding the healing process is an important element because each individual's healing journey is unique. I have had clients who have worked through the process very quickly, and there have been clients who have taken longer to heal. This element encourages *progression* and not *perfection*. Some people do not notice how much they have healed until they look back at themselves after six months and realise that they are different people. They may still face the same obstacles but something within them has changed.

Element 3: Tools for emotional healing

The third element outlines the tools required to propel the healing process. It is important to recognise that these tools *do not do the healing themselves*, but rather they promote the healing process. As you start to introduce these factors into your life you will realise that your perception will slowly begin to change and you will begin to act in accordance with your true selves. The tools expand your awareness as well as put you in touch with both the individual and transcendent part of yourselves.

I have mentioned previously that the Transcendent Healing Process addresses our paradoxical natures and this is why it promotes a deeper healing. These tools alone may not yield the deeper healing that you require because they function from the level of the mind. These tools are *things that you can do* and *ways in which you can behave*, and they have the power to help you immensely. However, we must remember that our individual mind itself plays a crucial role in the formation of emotional wounding; hence our individual mind cannot *entirely* facilitate the healing itself. Many people can see what they are doing wrong and they try their absolute best to change their behaviour, and yet despite their efforts they still continue the same behaviour and often experience a deep sense of confusion and incessant mind chatter. In some cases people feel it is necessary to temporarily take anti-depressants in order to calm the mind chatter.

The individual mind is only part of who we are and this is why traditional therapy falls short for many people, because it only addresses the individual aspect of ourselves. My suggestion for you would be to use and work with these tools, but to keep in mind that they are only *part* of the healing process.

Element 4: The role of nutrition in emotional healing

The final element addresses our physical body and how it impacts our mind. Whilst there is often much that is said about the impact that the mind has on the body, it is also important to realise that the processes in the body also have an impact on the mind – sometimes enough to make an emotional ailment disappear completely. In fact, this is quite often one of the first factors that I explore when I work with clients - especially if they are working through depression or anxiety. I have now worked with a handful of clients who found that their anxiety completely disappeared after they changed their diet. One of these clients had suffered severely with anxiety since he was a teenager and after addressing his diet, he could not believe how much nutrition had affected his emotional wellbeing.

The food industry has changed dramatically over the years and processed foods have become the norm. We have seen an increase in many physical and emotional ailments and we cannot ignore the fact that we need to be vigilant about what we are putting into our bodies. Many of us do not stop to think about what impact the food is having on our physical and emotional wellbeing, and to make matters worse, lots of these foods promote addictive tendencies within us – to the extent that we become 'cranky' if we do not consume these items.

Therefore the forth element looks at the quality of food that we consume and how we can begin to take steps in order to promote a change in both our physical and emotional wellbeing.

5

The First Element: Emotional Wounding

The Transcendent Mind and Internal Dichotomies

We are *dichotomous* in nature and understanding how this dichotomy plays out in our life lays the foundation for emotional healing. According to the Oxford dictionary, the term dichotomy is *a division or contrast between two things that are represented as being opposed or entirely different.* For example, science and religion may be regarded as a dichotomy. The two disciplines are thought of as being entirely different, or even opposed. Science is based on facts, research findings and keeping an open mind, with careful consideration being given to limitations. Religion on the other hand, has been passed on through the ages and it is difficult to say to what degree the information is factual.

We experience dichotomy in many areas of our life and not understanding how to manage this is what creates an inner conflict. Here are some ways in which we personally experience dichotomy:

1)   We are both an individual mind and part of a Transcendent Mind, which means that we appear to be both separate and connected at the same time. This is the grandest dichotomy that we experience.

2)   We have both a 'head voice' which is the voice of reason, and 'heart voice' which is the voice of intuition.

3)   We are naturally designed to be authentic in our behaviour

but we are socially programmed to ignore this authenticity. Instead we are encouraged to be a certain way in order to 'fit in' with society.

4)   We have both a 'dark side' as well as a 'light side' to our personalities. This is why seemingly 'good' people sometimes do 'bad' things.

We don't just experience dichotomy as individuals but we also see it playing out in our environment. For example: night and day, hot and cold and up and down. The only difference is that nature's dichotomies don't create an issue for us because we accept them completely as a way of life.

The Greatest Dichotomy

Let us look at ourselves in more detail. To start with, I believe that each one of us is *dichotomous* at our very core. In other words, we are both an individual mind as well as being part of the Transcendent Mind. This is the grandest dichotomy that we experience. All other personal dichotomies that we encounter in our lives stem from this foundation.

Our individual mind allows us to exist in our own unique way, and to make our own decisions. It allows us the freedom to make the all-important choice: that when responding to what life brings, will we choose the path of love, or will we choose the path of fear? Traditional psychotherapy works with our individual mind, helping us to become more aware and make more conducive choices. It doesn't however, fully address the question of who we are beyond our individual consciousness and this is why it is only partially effective.

Beyond our individual consciousness, we are part of a Transcendent Mind. So far we have explored aspects of this mind. We know that we're all connected via the Transcendent Mind, but we also know that love, compassion, kindness and empathy are what connect us as human beings. These are feelings that we can't measure, yet are felt powerfully. It is the feeling of compassion and empathy that we experience for one another that creates transformational change in society. As I write this today, the situation between the Israelis and Palestinians is delicate, with a lot of innocent lives being lost. Yesterday, one of clients phoned up and said that she needed to postpone her therapy session, as she was busy making sweet treats that she could sell. All the proceeds were going towards helping civilians who had been hurt in this conflict. My client is thousands of miles away from where the conflict is occurring, but yet feels compassion and empathy for the people who are suffering across the globe.

Deep down I believe that we are all *naturally* wired to express these expressions of love. It is important however, to recognise that *natural* does not necessarily mean *normal*. *Natural* is what we have been designed to do whereas *normal* is what we get into the habit of doing. For example, it is natural for us to express love, kindness and compassion towards others because ultimately we all function in the same way. We know what pain and loss feels like and hence we are able to relate to another's circumstance. However, normality can be different. Many individuals have been raised with an each-for-themselves attitude. I have lived close to Central London for most of my life and I am continually amazed to watch people on the trains. It can become very busy at times with people having no regard for one another. There is little acknowledgement and connection on this public transport system, as many people are engrossed in their own technological gadgets.

If however, we are all connected via the Transcendent Mind and if we are all wired naturally with tendencies such as love, compassion, kindness and empathy, then I believe that the language of the Transcendent mind is love. This is what connects us and this this what creates transformations in consciousness: a renewed sense of love for ourselves, love for others and love for our environment. We face challenges in life because somewhere within we face a deep inner conflict. There is a part of us feels that we are good, loving and connected to others. Many a time we hear ourselves saying that even though we've made mistakes, we're good people at heart. And that is the truth. Our natural nature is one of love.

The conflict is created however, because we have been conditioned to believe that we are *only* individual beings; and rather than listening to our hearts and following our calling we need to be making a living – even if it means doing something that we don't like doing. Rather than working together, we compete against one another. Rather than nurturing the creativity of each child, we label him or her when they don't fit into the academic system. We live in a state of fear: fear of not being good enough, fear of not having enough, fear of not being talented enough. *We have been conditioned to live in fear when our natural state is love, and this is what creates the deep inner conflict. This is the greatest dichotomy that we experience.* If we don't recognise this dichotomy playing out within us and if we don't recognise our true natures, how will we recognise the truth in another? If we don't learn how to forgive ourselves, how can we possibly forgive another? So understanding ourselves is the key, and this is why understanding our dichotomous nature and the Transcendent Mind is so important to emotional healing.

The Other Personal Dichotomies

Now that we have some understanding about our dichotomous natures - the fact that we are both individual and connected at the same time, we can deepen our understanding about the different ways in which this affects us.

Our Transcendent Mind knows the deeper purpose of life. It recognises that we are deeply connected at some level. I believe this is also where our 'gut instinct' comes from - that feeling that we get which may be against all the odds, but proves to be the correct decision in the end. Some time ago, I remember reading that Richard Branson strongly follows his gut instinct even if his advisors do not agree with his decision. I have also known of people who have avoided fatal motor accidents because they changed their usual route after getting a 'bad feeling' about it.

A while ago a friend of mine was on her way back to London from Leicester. She was bringing a friend back with her and by the time they reached London it was around 10.30pm. In order to get the passenger home, my friend had to drive a further twenty five minutes past her own house, so the overall journey was going to take her an extra fifty minutes. When they got into London and the passenger realised that my friend was going to drive her all the way home, she insisted that would be fine taking a train home for the rest of the journey. However, my friend told her that it was too late to take the train and that she would rather drop her home to ensure that her safe return. Upon hearing this, the passenger told my friend that she *really* was a nice person; to which my friend replied, "it's not that I am a nice person, it is just that I do the right thing".

Many of us can relate to this circumstance, where we have travelled an exhausting long journey and want nothing more than to be home, curled up on our sofa with a hot chocolate and our favourite movie. However, we have made that extra journey because deep down we know it is the right thing to do, we choose to act out of empathy and compassion over our exhaustion. In these cases we're following our true inner guidance. (I will discuss more about this later in the book, as even in these circumstances there is a balance to be achieved).

The Transcendent Mind is also the inner voice that we don't want to hear at times. The voice that tells us that our current relationship is failing and we need to leave; it is also the voice that tells us that even though we may be in a really well paid job, it is time for us to reconsider our career path so that we are able to follow our inner calling. The Transcendent Mind is our inner guide and if we listen to it, it will keep us on the correct path. It is the 'light' side of us – the authentic side of us. The only issue is that sometimes courage is required to act upon this guidance.

We also have within us the complete opposite of our light side. We have within us our dark side too and this is what forms the dichotomy. The dark side stems from the belief that we separate beings. If you remember, our *natural* state is one of love and connectedness, but we grow up believing that we are individual in every sense. This creates an uncomfortable void within us that plays out in a number of ways. In some cases the manifestation can be quite self-destructive, such as people engaging in alcoholism or self-harm to a degree where it severely affects the quality of their life. In other cases it may not be as apparent and it may manifest perhaps as a subtle constant undertone of loneliness, frustration or depression.

Growing up, I was a well-behaved child. I was considered to be intelligent by the current academic standards and I was also emotionally mature for my age. As I got into my early-twenties, my life seemed perfect from the outside. I had a good job, I was getting married and settling down and life was good. However, what people didn't know (even those closest to me), was that I had battled an eating disorder for a majority of my life because I was able to hide it well. Up until my mid-twenties no-body was able to tell because I had managed to keep my weight and public eating behaviour in check. However, when I got into my mid-twenties I was unable to keep up the internal conflict and the eating disorder spiralled out of control, resulting in substantial weight gain. And of course with the weight gain came insensitive comments from family and friends, which gave my self-esteem a further battering to the point that I stopped socialising completely. In fact, some of my family did not get to see me for a five-year period. I remember wondering how such an intelligent, nice, successful girl had become someone who was overweight and battling with her relationship with food, socially recluse and in a marriage that was on the verge of breaking down. I was still that nice girl; it was only that my dark side was playing out heavily because I hadn't yet learned how to manage my physical, emotional and spiritual life effectively.

It was only when I started my own journey to recovery and internal exploration that I realised that both the light and the dark existed within me, and my job was to learn how to manage these aspects. I also realised that the people who judged me did not yet recognise the truth about who they were either. We can only treat a person as far as we have come in our personal development. If we haven't yet learned how to be compassionate and forgiving towards ourselves, then we may not be able to extend these qualities to another. In other words, if we have not owned up to and accepted our own darkness, then we will find it difficult to accept the dark side of another.

Authenticity is another area within us that gives rise to a dichotomy. Rachel had been privately educated from a young age. Being part of large family, she had encountered many issues whilst growing up. However, her parents provided her with material wealth and gifted her an excellent education. Rachel was highly intelligent and excelled in most subjects at school. She secured a place at a good university where she studied a degree in economics. After university and much to her parents' delight, she landed a good job working a tax inspector. There was only one problem: Rachel absolutely detested the job. During the four years she spent fulfilling the role, she gradually found herself falling into a state of depression. Life had lost its spark and Rachel was miserable.

Rachel had arrived at an interesting junction in her life. On one hand she was desperately seeking the approval of her parents, and the role as a tax inspector was fulfilling this void. Her parents were immensely proud of her, as their investment in her education had paid off. But deep down Rachel was attracted to working with teens and young adults. She had a burning desire to make a real difference in the lives of young people in a fun way. She also had a natural entrepreneurial streak and desperately wanted to bring these two areas of passion together. Eventually Rachel decided to quit her role as a tax inspector, but unfortunately she lost the respect of her family too. She was no longer the intelligent, high-achieving daughter. She was now perceived as someone who had lost her way and wasted her education. She had gone from earning an excellent wage to earning basic rate pay, and was constantly reminded of how she had failed in life. Rachel soon started to believe the people around her and both her self-confidence and esteem plummeted. She no longer considered herself to be worthy and intelligent; rather she had become so full of fear that she could no longer feel her own authenticity.

It took a while to work with Rachel and we slowly started to peel back the layers of pain that had accumulated within her. She realised that she had many unresolved issues with certain family members, and she started to understand the power of forgiveness, compassion and acceptance. She also began to understand the concept of healthy boundaries and the fact that her thoughts and opinions were worth something. Although it took her a couple of years, she slowly started to progress towards expressing her authenticity in every area of her life. She knew that she would never feel completely fulfilled in a finance-based career, so she took the step to start right at the bottom in a education-based career instead. All the while she continued to work on herself. In time, various areas of her life started to heal. She began to understand her family from a place of compassion, and she worked tirelessly to improve her financial situation. She grew stronger as she continued to express her authenticity, and just recently she purchased her first educational franchise.

Like many others, Rachel experienced the dichotomy of authenticity strongly. Left unresolved, this dichotomy would have caused her much suffering throughout life. If Rachel had chosen to ignore her gut instinct and if she had stayed in a job where she was miserable, Rachel's quality of life and emotional wellbeing would have suffered severely. But by taking the courageous steps to address this major conflict that she was experiencing within, Rachel turned her life around. She transcended the dichotomy.

Managing Dichotomies

By now you will have understanding of how dichotomies play out in our lives. One of the keys to emotional healing is learning how to manage your internal dichotomies. It is about firstly becoming aware of your own inner conflicts and having strategies to deal with them, and secondly recognising the grander truth about your mind. If we want to heal emotionally, we need to start taking steps towards uncovering our *natural* natures and we also need to begin thinking and behaving in ways that allow us to express who we truly are. Element three discusses how to manage dichotomies in more detail.

6

The First Element: Emotional Wounding
The Individual Self

James was shy child, softly spoken and very well behaved. At the age of six, his parents separated. His father moved out the family home, leaving his mother distraught and struggling financially. Unable to cope with the separation James' mother started drinking alcohol regularly. She would often leave James home alone whilst she would go out socialising in the evenings. James quickly learned how to look after himself and over time he would often have to look after his mother too.

Although James had always been very good at art, he was forced to leave school at sixteen, as he had to work in order to look after himself. As the years went by James remained the shy type, finding it difficult to make friends and entertain romantic relationships. In his mid-twenties James' mother passed which led to him drinking heavily. James found that the drinking helped him to become more social but he also found that he would sometimes behave abusively whilst drunk. James would wake up each morning vowing to cut down on his alcohol intake, but each day he found himself in the same situation by the evening, hating himself a little more each time.

How Emotional Wounding Occurs

The previous chapters have illustrated that we are infinite and deeply connected at some level. I have put forward the notion that we belong to the Transcendent Mind, and that we suffer emotionally due to our internal dichotomies creating conflict within us. The aim of emotional healing however, is not to escape these dichotomies. We are both individual and deeply connected at the same time and it would be useless to try to change this truth because it forms the core of who we are.

We would not be able to experience life on Earth in the way that we do if this dichotomy did not exist, because it is our 'individual-ness' that ensures that we learn more about ourselves through relationships – this is how we learn to become better human beings. The 'individual' part of us provides us with the opportunity to express our oneness even though we appear to be separate. When we experience dislike for somebody else and want to fix the issue, we first have to look within and work on ourselves. We need to develop the *ability* to forgive or see things from their perspective if we wish to make our lives easier.

In order to be able to better ourselves as people, we first need to understand why we function the way we do. So far in this book, we have considered the bigger picture, but now I would like to share with you how the individual part of us develops.

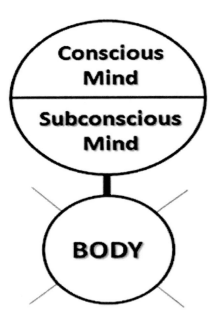

Dr. Thurman Fleet created this visual representation of the mind (the stickperson) in the 1930s. The reason the head appears to be bigger than the body is because the mind is commonly considered to be in the head, and it is the mind that controls the body. The body on its own is a mere manifestation of what is going on in the mind.

The top part of the mind represents the conscious mind. This is also known as our 'thinking mind'. It is where we make all our decisions. For example when we decide what to wear or what to eat, we are utilising our conscious mind.

The bottom part of the mind represents our subconscious mind. The subconscious element of our mind is more powerful than the conscious part, and is in fact responsible for most of the activity in our daily lives. This part of our mind already has survival instincts etched into it when we are born. As we begin to grow, our conscious mind starts to develop and picks up messages through our physical senses, which are filtered through to the subconscious mind. Over time our experiences increase and the database grows. This creates our belief system. For example, if someone was continually told as a child that they were good for nothing and that they will never attain a good job, the child may grow up believing that this is the truth, and hence may not even attempt or entertain the idea of educating themselves well with the aim of getting a good job. Our thoughts give rise to our emotions and our emotions drive our actions, which determine the results that we produce.

As mentioned above, our subconscious mind has a survival instinct etched into it. This means that it will do whatever it can to keep us alive. One of the ways that it does this is that it records everything that we have done in the past that has taken away immediately, the emotional or physical pain that we have experienced. For example, if as a child we were given a cookie every time we hurt ourselves, then the subconscious mind relates the cookie to pain relief. We might find ourselves doing the same thing as we get older – using food to comfort ourselves emotionally. Similarly, in the example that I gave at the beginning of this chapter, James' mother started to consume alcohol regularly as it helped her deal with the emotional pain that she was suffering. The subconscious mind did not realise that the strategy was life threatening in the long term; it still continued to do what it had to in order to keep the emotional pain under control.

We can see from the example above that James was a shy child and was also a gifted artist. When his father left home, not only did James witness his mother's emotional pain, but he also had to grow up very quickly. There was an aspect of James that learned how to survive and look after himself. He was hard working and was prepared to do whatever it took in order to take charge of a situation. However, there was also a side of James that felt bitterness and resentment towards his mother. He was angry that he had to give up his childhood in order to become the adult in their relationship. He had not learned how to process his emotions effectively and felt that he couldn't integrate very well socially.

The messages that James received during his childhood had set the foundation for his adult experience and when his mother passed away, James turned to drinking – the only behaviour that he knew would lessen his pain momentarily. When James started therapy he said that he could not understand how a shy, gentle child had become an alcoholic, especially since alcoholism was the one thing that he detested.

Over time James learned how to express his feelings and he also understood the role that his mind had played in his situation. Slowly the resentment towards his parents started to heal as James started to understand that his parents had done the best that they could. Breaking free from the alcoholism was challenging for him because although it had started from his psychological issues, it had soon become a physiological issue too. In other words, not only did he have to address the emotional issues, but he also had to deal with the physical withdrawal symptoms that the body as experiencing.

Trapped Energy

Richard Flook, the founder of Advanced Clearing Energetics and author of Why Am I Sick? has been studying healing for the past 20 years. He states that:

- When we experience a trauma, the energy gets trapped in our body. Richard refers to these moments as UDIN moments, which are events that are unexpected, dramatic, isolating and ones that we have no strategy to deal with. When we experience a UDIN moment, the first place that the energy gets trapped is in the heart. This energy or emotion is then communicated to the gut, where it lodges. This stressful event then gets localised in the brain, in a specific area that relates embryonically to a part of an organ. The reaction of the organ is designed to assist you to solve the shock and learn from it.

- It is possible (via trained individuals), to ascertain one's complete disease history from a brain CT scan. Therefore a traumatic event not only causes emotional issues, but can cause physical diseases too.

- It has been shown that UDINs can be passed down the generations. These energetic shocks can be passed down from our parents to us. The shock is stored within us and may become activated at some point in our lives if we experience a UDIN moment. For example, a great-grandparent who experienced a famine passes down an expression of a gene that tells the body to overeat and store the excess energy whenever it can, in order to avoid death by starvation in the future. Fast-forward a few years: Let's say the parents of the great-grandchild limit the child's food for health reasons. This limitation may trigger the inherited gene's expression and cause the child to become clinically obese. [1]

I believe that emotional wounding occurs because of two reasons. The first is the trapped energy that is stuck within us. This may have come about either as a single traumatic event or, as subtler repeated experiences over a period of time through which we form our belief systems. There are a number of ways in which this trapped, stagnant energy can be shifted, for example through talking therapies, techniques such as the emotional freedom technique (EFT) or acupuncture.

The second reason for the occurrence of emotional wounding is not recognising and understanding that we are part of a Transcendent Mind. There is a healing that takes place beyond the shifting of stagnant energy. This is where we experience both the truth and depth of who we are. There is a sense of inner peace, inner contentment, a sense of belonging. It is a sense of wisdom, maturity in character, an integration of experiences that you are able to view from a renewed perspective. This is evident in some of the case studies that I have presented throughout this book, such as that of Mercedes Leal. We will take a closer look at the healing process in the next chapter.

With the above example, although James was making a good recovery, he got to a point where he still felt empty and a little lost. He knew how to change his thoughts so that he felt better emotionally - he was able to release most of the trapped energy within him; but he also started to question the purpose of life. This is when I introduced the concept of the Transcendent Mind to him and shared with him both research that had been conducted and case studies that had been recorded. We explored some of the spiritual texts and slowly James started to experience a higher level of awareness. He felt that he had gained a deeper understanding about life and started to look at situations differently. He commented that traditional therapy had helped him learn more about himself, but learning about the Transcendent Mind had put life into perspective for him. James understood that there was an internal place of peace forever within him and he could access it at any time.

I remember listening to an interview of the late Dr. David R. Hawkins in which he was explaining the nature of consciousness. He stated that the body had no capacity to experience itself and that it had to be experienced through the senses, and the senses had to be experienced in the mind. The mind too could not experience itself and hence had to be experienced in something greater than itself, which is consciousness. He went on to say that there was also a state beyond consciousness, which was *awareness*. Awareness is the stillness that allows us to be aware of what is going on in consciousness. Awareness is the energy of life itself, and this is what I refer to as the Transcendent mind.

Why The Transcendent Mind is Important for Emotional Healing

We are so programmed by everyday life that unless we are told, our conscious mind is not aware that it is part of something grander. The conscious mind is operating within the Transcendent Mind, and the Transcendent Mind is the fundamental truth of who we are.

When someone opts to go for therapy, they commonly encounter the popular psychotherapeutic models. Aside from building rapport and trust, these models mostly are still Newtonian in nature – especially the behaviour modification techniques. They work with the individual mind, looking for the cause and work on changing the thought. However, changing the thought alone is not always enough to heal emotionally. Often I come across people who understand intellectually that they need to change their thoughts to heal, they also understand that they have to let go of resentment and anger but they still find it difficult to do. This is because they have wounded hearts, and the mind alone cannot always heal a wounded heart.

Deeper healing involves a transformation of perception. As mentioned above, it involves shifting stagnant energy that has been stored within an individual. It also involves bringing love into the equation, and love of course is our natural language – the language of the Transcendent Mind. Love is what heals a wounded heart, and the individual mind is a tool that we use to help bring this state about.

Some time ago, Henry came to therapy with anger and control issues. He expressed that he was short-tempered and found it difficult to forgive. He also said that, even though he felt terrible afterwards, he tried to control situations to such an extent that it did not matter who he hurt in the process.

Once we had worked with the traditional psychotherapy methods for a while, I asked Henry whether he had any spiritual beliefs and I also introduced him to the concept of the Transcendent Mind. Henry told me that he had been very sensitive as a child and remembers having vivid dreams and visions between the ages of about five and eight years old. However, whilst growing up, he faced difficulties with the family and quickly developed a 'tough exterior'. His experiences left him angry and frustrated, with a deep need to control situations in order to avoid further emotional pain. I encouraged Henry to reconnect with his authentic self and address his emotions. Now that he was an adult, he had nothing to fear anymore and it was safe for him to be himself.

Like many others, from a young age Henry had felt that there was something more to people. A combination of his childhood dreams and visions, as well as personal spiritual beliefs led him to believe that we were spiritual beings having a human experience. Exploring the concept of a Transcendent Mind brought Henry much peace, and also a sense of validation as he realised that he was not alone in his thoughts.

Although it took time for Henry to work on his anger and control issues, exploring the Transcendent Mind had added a new dimension to his healing. In addition to working through his thoughts and feelings, he also worked on his spiritual connection. His awareness and personal connection to a bigger picture is what further propelled his emotional healing. He started recognising that we were all connected and this helped to develop his empathetic side, which in turn helped him to become less angry.

Death of the Ego

The death of the ego is the process that takes place during emotional healing and is an important part of consciousness transformation. As mentioned earlier in the book: the ego is the part of us that is *illusionary*. It is the part of us that has us believe that we're separate. The ego doesn't recognise that we're actually deeply interconnected and an integral part of the universe. Obviously, we have separate bodies and individual minds, but we are also part of something much greater. When we believe that we are nothing other than our separate selves, it can be easy to be selfish, angry, greedy and inconsiderate towards those around us. After all, what motivation do we have to be loving towards one another? Instead we take the attitude that this is our life and that we need to do whatever we can to survive. Rather than coming together and collaborating with one another, we choose the path of competition. A world that believes that it is made up of separate beings not connected in any way, is a world that finds it hard to forgive and move on. It is also a world that operates on the basis of conditional love. How can a world with this belief system possibly create a truly peaceful existence?

Our ego is our inability to live in the present moment. When we're stuck in the past or entirely focussed on the future, we are operating from our ego. Many people think that they need to kill the ego off completely in order to live a happier life, but I feel that awareness is the key. Although our ego is responsible for our negative intents and actions, it is still useful to an extent because it enables us to integrate into this Earthly experience. Not being aware of the ego intensifies the dichotomies that we experience and causes a hindrance to personal growth, but becoming aware of the ego enables us to recognise the dichotomies that are playing out in our lives. Awareness allows us to see the truth and choose a different response. Becoming aware of the ego also connects us to the part of ourselves that transcends the ego. The Transcendent Mind is a deeper dimension within us that recognises the ego. This is the part of us that begins to realise that the ego is playing up, and it silently observes. We are both the observer and the observed. In the example above, Henry's anger and control issues started to subside when he began to observe his mind and the thoughts that were going through it. He also started to experience glimpses of inner stillness as he connected with the present moment, and in time he started to choose different responses.

In Henry's case (and in the case of many others), emotional healing takes time. However, for a few people the shift in perception is instant because they experience the truth about who they really are. They encounter the feeling of true joy and deep love and in that instant they realise the truth, and they feel the interconnectedness. This is what happened with Anita Moorjani, the lady who had the near-death experience and the miraculous healing from cancer. However, this does not necessarily mean that the individual stays in that higher state of consciousness all the time, but rather they drift in and out of it, and have the ability to view life from a different perspective.

I want to mention here a little bit about near-death states and what they can contribute to our personal emotional healing. By now, it should be clear that:

1) We have an individual mind but we are also part of a greater Transcendent Mind.

2) Traditional therapy is Newtonian in its approach, meaning that it deals with cause and effect. In a nutshell, it works on building rapport, exploring the past and, behaviour modification.

3) We *need* to move beyond traditional therapy. In order to heal

effectively we *need* to further understand who we are at the core. We *need* to take into consideration the current research that has been conducted in the field and we *need* to recognise what this means for us.

4) We are naturally designed to express traits such as love, compassion, kindness and empathy. However, our perceptions are blinded by misguided beliefs.

The field of near death studies is an important point of consideration as it can involve a transformation of consciousness. In 2004, The Journal of Near Death Studies published the work of Bruce Greyson and Kenneth Ring: *The Life Changes Inventory – Revised*. The paper highlights that psychological and behavioural changes are well recognised after effects of near death experiences. The paper states:

Near –death experiences are profound subjective experiences with mystical or transcendent features that some people report to have occurred during the course of a close brush with death… Characteristic psychological and behavioural changes are now well recognised as after effects of NDEs. These changes typically include an enhanced appreciation for everyday life. Greater feelings of self-worth and self-acceptance, compassionate concern for others, reverence for all forms of life and a heightened sensitivity to the ecological health of the planet, devaluation of materialistic acquisitions, devaluation of competitive striving against others, a universal and inclusive spirituality, tremendous thirst for knowledge, conviction that life is meaningful, elimination of fear of death, conviction of sustained consciousness after death, and the certainty of the existence of an ultimate, divine being. [2]

It seems that some near-death experiencers undergo a transformation of consciousness. It is interesting to note that some of the factors mentioned in the above quote, such as an appreciation for everyday life and greater feelings of self-worth and self-acceptance, are the same results that we look to achieve through therapy. The difference being that therapy may take a while as the person's perception changes over time. I feel that some near-death experiencers go through swifter transformations in consciousness because they encounter the truth about who they really are. They experience the death of the ego during their near-death state and hence their beliefs systems fall away, revealing their true identity. Their experience changes their view about reality as we know it.

In her book, *The Big Book of Near Death Experiences*, Dr. Atwater shares an experience of Mellen-Thomas Benedict, a thirty-three year old male who suffered from an inoperable brain tumour. Dr. Atwater writes:

Mellen-Thomas Benedict, California; thirty-three years old, inoperable brain tumour: During my interview session with him, Mellen-Thomas told me that he had once been an accomplished lighting/cameraman for feature films and had racked up a lifetime of major events before he was thirty. Retiring from the frenzied world of filmdom, he moved to Fayetteville, North Carolina, to be near his parents and operate a stained-glass studio. That's when the diagnosis was made: cancer. His condition worsened rapidly. One morning, he awakened knowing that he would die that day, and he did. As a typical heaven-like scenario began to unfold, Mellen-Thomas recognised what was happening as it was happening!

Just as he reached the light at the end of the tunnel, he shouted, "stop a minute. This is my death and I want to think about this." By consciously intervening, he willfully changed his near-death scenario into an exploration of realms beyond imagining, a complete overview of history from the Big Bang to four hundred years into the future.

Then he was pulled through the light away from the tunnel, far away from Earth, past stars and galaxies, past imagery and physical realities, to a multi-angled overview of all worlds and all Creation, and past even that to a second light at the edge of existence where vibrations cease. He saw all wars from their beginnings, race as personality clusters, species operating like cells in a greater whole.

By merging into the matrix of his soul, he confronted the 'NO THING' from which all things emerge. Mellen-Thomas saw planetary energy systems in detail and how human thoughts influence these systems in a simultaneous interplay between past, present and future. He learned that Earth is a great cosmic being. He was aware of "falling" back into his body after deciding to return from his journey; as near as his hospice caretaker could determine, his experience took about ninety minutes. His doctor's assessment, though was the most shocking – the cancer he had once had had completely vanished.

"Because this happened to me my fear is gone, and my perspective has changed. You know, we are a very young species. The violence that formed the earth is in us too. As the earth is mellowing, so are we as people. Once pollution slows, we will reach a period of sustained consciousness. We have evolved as life forms from single-celled organisms to complex structures, and finally to a global brain. Employment levels will never be again as they once were, which will force a redefinition of human rights. We will adopt a more nurturing type of consciousness, freeing the mind for exceptional achievement. I now know that all the answers to the world's problems are just beneath the surface in US ALL. Nothing is unsolvable."

Since his experience, Mellen-Thomas Benedict has been flooded with ideas for inventions and the marketing plans necessary to promote them. He has been granted a number of U.S patents and is actively engaged in advanced DNA research on the frontiers of science." [3]

The Ultimate Question: Why are we here?

The first element is important because it sets the foundation for emotional healing. Whilst tools such as: exploring, talking and releasing stuck energy are important for the healing process; understanding *who* we are at the core and *how* we function provides the bigger picture. This awareness is what helps us to change perspective, and a change in perspective is what propels healing. Although many of us will not have had near-death or out-of-body experiences, we still have the rich anecdotal evidence (from those who have experienced this phenomena), to learn from. As we sought to explore our true natures, we will realise that in fact we know very little about ourselves.

Aside form questioning who we are and how we function, perhaps the greatest mystery of all is *why* we are here? Why are we having this experience on Earth? Are we just a part of evolution, or is there a deeper reason for our incarnation? Questioning the reason for our existence is a necessary part of the emotional healing puzzle because for many, it provides a purpose. Quite often when we ask the deeper questions in life, we have to refer to philosophy and spirituality to provide a perspective, especially since conventional science has not yet reached a point of definite conclusion.

Many of the people that I work with believe in a higher entity – God. Of course there are different interpretations for this term, but generally most individuals seem to agree on one point: that God is an all-encompassing higher entity. Sometimes I meet people who are suffering emotionally because they do not understand how they fit into the grander scheme of things, and they cannot bring themselves to accept that life finishes when we die. As a Higher Entity plays a part in the life of so many, it makes sense to explore how we can incorporate this into healing.

I have mentioned before that healing needs to be addressed on three levels: body, mind and spirit. We are comfortable with using nutrition and traditional therapy to work with the body and the mind, but how do we address the spirit? To begin with, we need to have an understanding of what the spirit (or soul) is, and interestingly enough, most faiths and spiritual texts talk about the soul. *The Bible* refers to it as the Holy Spirit, as does *A Course in Miracles*. The Holy Spirit is the God within us, our true essence that is there to provide us personal guidance. It is the source of our intuition and our expressions of love, kindness, empathy and forgiveness.

According to the Upanishads, Brahman is the spirit supreme – the energy of the universe and beyond. He[10] is both the transcendent and the imminent, and the therefore he is the Self that resides within us: the Observer, the Atman, the Holy Spirit. This is why religious texts state that God is not 'out-there', but rather should be sought within ourselves, for there is a place within us where Brahman resides. The Bible too states that *the kingdom of God is within you.*

---

10   Brahaman is often referred to as a male energy.

It is said in the *Chandogya Upanishad* that the body ages, grows old and dies. But, the Brahman within us cannot die, it is *beyond* sorrow, grief, evil and hunger; The Brahman within is love and the voice of truth. It is our soul.

In order to heal we must find our soul. This is the purpose of life. This is why we are here: *to recognise who we truly are, to transcend our egos and unite with Brahman – what I refer to as the Transcendent Mind.* Once we have found our soul and recognised the Brahman within us, emotional wounding no longer exists. This is how miraculous healings occur and this is also why the there are reports of blind people being able to see during their near-death experiences. Deep healings occur when we recognise that the Supreme Soul and we are one.

The Upanishads also discuss the difference between the body and the soul (atman): The body is mortal and will inevitably at some point, meet death. The soul however is the immortal element that resides within the body. The body is influenced by pain and pleasure, and hence when an individual is attached to their body alone, they will always be bound by pain or pleasure. They will not be free to transcend this state because they will not yet have realised that they have a soul within.

As the soul within us is the Brahman – the spirit supreme, it is considered to be the source of infinite joy, love and truth. When an individual recognises their soul as free, immortal and able to exist beyond the body; it is then that the individual has attained true freedom. Our body is merely an organ through which our soul perceives. When we 'see' something, it is the soul that is seeing. The eyes are only the organ through which the soul sees. Similarly, when we 'feel' something' it is the soul that is feeling. The soul is Brahman, Supreme Consciousness, the Holy Spirit and the Transcendent mind, and this is where the experience occurs.

According to the Upanishads, the soul is not recognised through the intellect or through reasoning, and nor is it attained through sacred teaching. The soul is experienced in a place beyond thought. When we consider emotional wounding from a spiritual or soul perspective, we come to realise the primary reason for the existence of emotional wounding:

Not recognising our true purpose and true identities as souls is what creates an emotionally wounded heart.

Once we recognise this truth, we realise that all other emotional suffering stems from this. If we were all raised with the understanding, (or at the very least exposed to), the concept of a Transcendent Mind and the mind, body and spirit connection, then emotional suffering would not be experienced at the level at which it is today. Yes, we would still feel uncomfortable emotions, but we would be better equipped to handle them. We would know that each of us are equal at the very core, we would respect one another's divinity. We would be comfortable in our bodies and accept our differences. We would take back our personal power and step into expressing the magnificence of whom we really are. We would be more compassionate and we would place the life of another human above profit. We would work in collaboration and not in competition and we would strive to attain a sense of deep inner contentment. Quite simply, we would move away from a culture that focuses on serving just ourselves and our immediate families, and we would move towards seeing the divine in all. If we all focussed on serving one another, then nobody would remain in lack because there would always be somebody there to help.

In order to materialise this sort of a society, we first have to work on raising individual consciousness, which starts with working on ourselves. Before looking at the wrongdoing of another and judging them, we must first address ourselves. We must become aware of our emotional wounds and we must look to heal these, not only for ourselves but also for our future generations, for what we do not address, our children will inherit.

Element One Summary

- We are dichotomous in nature: we are both an individual mind as well as being part of the Transcendent Mind.

- We need to move beyond traditional therapy if we wish to experience a deeper healing.

- Emotional wounding occurs as a result of two reasons: firstly due to trapped energy which is the result of emotional pain and trauma; and secondly due to not understanding that we are part of a Transcendent Mind. Emotional wounding at its core is *not recognising our true purpose and identity as souls.*

- In order to heal we must find our souls, address our egos and pay attention to our bodies.

- We are naturally designed to express traits such as love, compassion, empathy and forgiveness.

- In order to materialise a society of higher consciousness, we must first work on ourselves, what we don't heal our children will inherit.

7

The Second Element: Emotional Healing
The Healing Process

A few months prior to coming to therapy, one of my clients, Jasmine had a conversation with a colleague at work about how she felt lost, and at the same time convinced that there was something 'bigger' out there. Her colleague, having previously entertained the idea of consciousness in his personal life, told her that perhaps she needed to look deeper within to find some answers.

Over the next couple of months, Jasmine continued to think about the conversation and eventually when things in her personal life became harder to handle, she decided to contact me. Jasmine came to therapy with what seemed like (from her perspective), predominantly a relationship issue. After a brief chat it came to light that Jasmine felt that she needed answers to many questions. She was tired of observing the same repetitive pattern that life would manifest for her.

She realised that deep down she believed herself to be a victim and felt that she had always had issues with female relationships in her life. This time, Jasmine was having an issue with one of her friends, Kate - whom she felt was mistreating her. Not an overly social person, Jasmine was afraid of losing the small group of friends that she had. She also felt sad at the fact that she had not been in a romantic relationship with someone in over five years.

Therapy helped Jasmine to work through these issues. Over time she started to speak her truth with Kate, and also explore her own authenticity, and she found that life began to open its doors for her. Within weeks of expressing herself and working on becoming more authentic, Jasmine realised that her relationships were beginning to change for the better and Kate was no longer contacting her. Not only that, shortly afterwards she met a wonderful man who cared and nurtured her in the right way and for the first time in years, Jasmine felt a sense of inner contentment.

A few months after experiencing improved relationships, I received a phone call from her. She explained that she had recently experienced the most beautiful overwhelming feeling of compassion for her best friend Kate whilst driving. She said that this experience had taken her by surprise because firstly, she hadn't thought about Kate in some time, and secondly, although she no longer viewed herself as a victim, Jasmine wasn't yet in a place where she had compassion for Kate either - saying that she had 'neutral' feelings about the situation. Finally, Jasmine expressed that she wasn't even sure if it was possible for her to ever feel pure love and compassion for Kate in the way in which she did.

However, after experiencing that overwhelming feeling in the car that day, Jasmine said she felt as if her heart was beginning to heal. She also shared that it wasn't an experience that she could put into words, only that the healing went beyond the mind.

Retrospectively looking at her healing, Jasmine said that she couldn't quite put her finger on how and why she had healed, but she did recognise a few things about the change. Although she had no prior knowledge about it, she said that when we explored the topic of consciousness, there was something familiar about our discussions. In other words, she knew deep down that she was part of something grander, that life wasn't just about her physical body and her mind. Equipped with this knowledge, she felt that she had to break the pattern of making poor relationship choices and that she had to start taking steps, that although she found painful, knew were in her best interest — she had to stop playing the victim. Also, exploring consciousness made her realise that she couldn't control all of life's circumstances and that ultimately she had to develop a trust in life - that if she took the most positive steps, life would certainly reciprocate.

Jasmine had to learn to connect to her authenticity and this did not reside in her conscious mind. She had to go beyond the conscious mind to connect with her deeper self. Exploring consciousness meant that she entertained the concept of the soul and what this meant for her. She had to learn to listen to her heart, and although it wasn't always what she wanted to hear, she knew that it was the truth.

One of the most important observations that Jasmine made was that her healing wasn't a linear A-B-C process and she couldn't always describe in words how and what had changed within. She felt (like so many others who have walked the path of deep healing), that first she understood intellectually the idea of the soul and consciousness, and although deep down it felt true to her, she said that the healing didn't occur until she was able to internalise the concept. Her healing came about when her feelings changed, but she couldn't quite describe how this had happened – only that it had taken time and had felt as if her heart had opened up. This is not something that she could have achieved with her mind alone.

Emotional Healing

The truth of the matter is that I don't know *exactly how* emotional healing occurs –especially in cases where the healing would be considered as being miraculous. However, I have spent a few years observing both my own healing experiences as well as the experiences of others, and in this element I will share with you what I know:

There are Different Levels of Healing

For most people, emotional healing is an on-going process and occurs gradually over time. We go through a process of recognising and removing layers of programming and false beliefs that have built up over the years. In chapter six I said that emotional wounding was the result of two reasons: the first was trapped energy, and the second was not recognising that we are part of a Transcendent Mind. The healing process therefore, reflects these two factors. Over the years, I have observed two main types of healing that takes place: *specific healing* and *deeper healing*.

Specific healing is a healing that occurs in response to a specific issue, for example, binge eating disorder. It is possible to heal binge eating disorder using a range of different techniques and healing modalities. We can address the person's physiology and psychology and help the person to manage the issue. But, it is important to realise that although the person may have managed or healed the binge eating disorder, they may not have undergone a deep shift in perception. In other words, they will have addressed certain aspects of the mind and the body, but they will not have experienced a deeper healing. This is why some individuals still may feel a sense of emptiness once their specific issue has been healed. This is also why we sometimes encounter people who consider themselves fortunate in every way, and yet still experience a void.

The second type of healing is a *deeper healing*. This is when a person has a deep shift in perception and sees the world differently. This type of healing may occur gradually or instantaneously, and (in some cases), people find it difficult to integrate back into daily life. Deeper healing produces a shift in the very core of a person, and it can occur at anytime. As mentioned in the previous chapter, this does not necessarily mean that the individual stays in that higher state of consciousness all the time, but rather they drift in and out of it, and have the ability to view life from a different perspective.

It is also possible for a person to experience this deeper healing but still struggle with specific healing issues. In fact, I believe this happened to me. I started to experience a deeper healing whilst I was still struggling with binge eating disorder. I required a different set of skills to heal that particular issue. This can also manifest in reverse as well, where sometimes I work with people who heal their specific issues, but choose to continue coming in for a session occasionally because they feel a deeper healing taking place. They are not always sure how or why this healing is occurring, but they say that exploring the multi-disciplinary perspective that I share with them helps. Through a combination of specific and deeper healing, the 'whole' (mind, body and spirit), of an individual is addressed. I believe that many experience a change in perception eventually, and at some point they start to question the deeper purpose of life.

We can feel that a change has taken place as our hearts begin to heal and when we begin to recognise who we really are. It happens as we start to correct our perceptions about ourselves, others, and the environment around us. We know that a healing is occurring when love, compassion, kindness and unity begin to fill our hearts. We are able to view life's challenges through a fresh perspective as we begin to experience a greater level of inner peace.

There is No Single Method to Attain Healing

The journey to healing is unique to every individual. There is no single method to achieve emotional healing, but rather there are many different routes that people can take. Some of the people that I have worked with have experienced the onset of healing through their religion, whereas for others the process has started though therapy or entertaining the notion that they are a soul. There are also people for whom the transformation has started because they have connected with something that someone has said, or through a movie that they have watched, or even through witnessing great suffering first hand. *A Course in Miracles* states that psychotherapy and religion are both experiences, and at their highest levels they become one. Neither of them is the truth, but both of them can lead to the truth. They are paths; avenues for the conscious mind to take that will stimulate the mysterious process of a deeper healing.

People often question why they experience emotional suffering and they ask why life presents them with challenging circumstances. I tell them that it is these challenging circumstances that give us the opportunity to grow as individuals. When life forces us into a corner, we have no option other than to change our perception and learn more about ourselves. We may also find ourselves becoming more compassionate towards other people who experience similar obstacles. If on the other hand, we choose not to change, we will continue to face similar challenges throughout life. Also, for some of us, emotional suffering is necessary so that we can rise to fulfil our life's calling. I have had to do a tremendous amount of work on myself to be able to work with others, so for me my darkest times eventually became my greatest gift.

Healing can be Instantaneous or Gradual

As mentioned earlier, there are few people that experience an instantaneous healing. It is as if somebody has removed a blindfold from their eyes and they are now able to see clearly. They understand the grander purpose of life and their priorities change. Life may become more service-focussed, and sometimes these individuals can have difficulty integrating back into normal daily life.

For most people however, emotional healing takes time and can often be a process of taking two steps forward followed by one step backwards. The change is gradual - but also apparent when one looks back after a period of time. Frequent challenges will still occur, but eventually our way of dealing with them changes. It is not a process that can be forced or rushed, but rather one that comes about at its own pace.

Intention and Allowing

Emotional healing is a combination of *intention* and *allowing*. Over the years, I have made an interesting observation about the healing process: there is only a certain amount of healing that we can do ourselves through our conscious mind; the rest of the healing happens via the Transcendent Mind and is an unconscious process. Sometimes it does not matter how much we have the *desire* to heal, the healing happens in its own time. The desire to heal quite often stems from the mind, but the healing itself takes place at a deeper level, and it is not a process that we can force. The Transcendent Mind is the energy within us that is already healed. Throughout the ages, people have used different terms to refer to this energy: Holy Spirit, Paramatman; the God within us; Love. This is a different *state* to the conscious mind. The conscious mind operates from a limited state. It worries and tries to control situations, and looks for solutions to problems. It tries to bring about a healing change through thought alone, but most often our deep-rooted feelings surface, making the change difficult. Conventional therapy works with the conscious mind.

The Transcendent Mind however, operates from an *enlightened* state, and is often subtle in the way in which it works. Our task is to use our conscious minds to initiate and open up to the healing that the Transcendent Mind offers. Our job is to relax and call upon the Transcendent Mind to continue the healing, and through this process we intend to experience the truth of who we really are. We do not know in our ordinary, limited conscious state when this healing will occur and neither can we predict the process of the method through which it will come about.

As mentioned previously, emotional healing takes place when love fills our heart, and although we can take practical steps (such as learning behaviour modification techniques) to initiate the healing process, this does not necessarily fill our heart with love. Behaviour modification techniques take place in our mind, and the deeper healing that I talk about in this book takes place in every cell of our body. It is rather like the journey that science has taken over the years: the journey from Newtonian science to the quantum world, the journey of a predictable outcome to an unexplainable outcome. There comes a point when a greater energy propels the healing.

Unless instantaneous and completely unexpected, emotional healing is often a combination of *intention* and *allowing*. Having the desire and then intention to heal initiates the healing process. When we recognise that emotional suffering is affecting us on many levels, and when this pain becomes unbearable, we make the choice to change. This is a necessary step because it opens our minds up to the positive changes to come. We start to look for ways in which we can feel better and we try different healing modalities, connecting with ones that suit us the most. We begin to learn about the impact that our thoughts have on both our physical and emotional wellbeing. We question our behaviour and where possible, we begin to change our responses.

The *intention* aspect of healing involves conscious thought and action. It is the 'doing' part of the healing process – the part that we initiate through our free will. However, coming from the limited conscious part of our minds, these actions are limited in their ability to heal us fully. This is where conventional therapy hits a roadblock and this is the reason why I see individuals coming into my clinic who have tried everything, are fully ready and willing, but are still suffering.

The second ingredient necessary for emotional healing is the *allowing* process, which as the name states, is when we *allow* the healing process to occur. At the beginning of this section I mentioned that I did not know exactly how the emotional healing occurs. I know what the results are and I am aware of steps that we can take in order to promote emotional healing, but I do not know of the exact mechanism that takes place when the healing occurs. What I do know is that the Transcendent Mind is at work during this process, and I also know that being in a state of relaxation, joy and detachment from the outcome aids this process.

I am aware that it sounds almost contradictory to be detached from the outcome (which is emotional wellbeing), when healing is what you intended in the first place. However, attachment to the outcome and worrying about whether the healing will occur or not, serves as a distraction from relaxation. It creates noise in the conscious mind and may set up a resistance to the healing itself. Therefore relaxation, joy, detachment and faith are necessary aspects that help the *allowing* phase of the healing to take place.

The Four-Phase Healing Process

To explore the healing process in further detail, let us take a look at the following four-step process. It is important to realise that this process does not always occur in a linear fashion. They are many cases where the steps overlap, or even where individuals move between steps repetitively. For example, it is not unusual for a person to experience steps 1, 2 and 3 and then return back to step 1 again at a later stage. This four-step process that I have outlined is general representation of how the overall healing process is experienced for both specific and deeper healing.

- **Phase 1: Intention and Exploration**

    As explained above, during this process the individual opens up to the idea of emotional healing. This often happens when we experience difficult circumstances in life and decide that it is time to get some help.

    During this phase, one expresses an intention to heal and begins to work through their thoughts and feelings. For many people, this process alone can provide much relief as they begin to talk openly (in a safe environment) about things that they may have been bothering them for a while. People will really begin to connect with their feelings and will start to process any pain if they need to. They also begin to reflect upon and question their thoughts and behaviour. Many of them may begin to develop a heightened level of awareness.

    Quite often during this phase I may explore an individual's spiritual beliefs and share additional research and information with them. We also look at practical steps if they are required - this is entirely dependent on the individual and their unique circumstance. Some people prefer only conventional therapeutic methods, whereas others choose a deeper level of exploration. I believe that this whole process propels a deeper level of healing.

- **Phase 2: Being, Relaxation and Allowing**

    An individual experiences a different state of consciousness during this phase of healing. In phase 1, a whole array of emotions may be experienced. A person may feel anything from relief to anger, or even extreme stress and pain. But this second phase is about relaxation and *being*.

Sometimes I will introduce aspects of this phase simultaneously to phase 1, but this all depends on the person that I am working with. This phase is all about learning how to relax and 'being' in the present moment: It is about stopping to experience the space that you are in and breathing and connecting with your breath. It is about allowing yourself to just experience the present moment no matter what is happening. Here you connect with life: no matter how busy you are or how bad you perceive your situation to be, just for one moment, allow yourself to be ok with where you are. Allow yourself the space, the time and the gift to stop, breathe and relax.

This phase is very different from *doing*. It is not about 'doing' anything to achieve a particular result. It is not about thinking about your thoughts and correcting them and it is not about 'thinking' to find solutions. This phase is about *being*, which involves experiencing the present moment – good or bad. It is about realising that nothing lasts forever, and it is about having faith that the Transcendent Mind is healing you as you are *being*.

The only *doing* that I encourage in this phase is doing things that bring a sense of joy. It could be anything that you enjoy doing: reading a book, cooking, making cards, playing an instrument, building something, colouring-in, doing a jigsaw puzzle, socialising with friends, going for a walk, listening to music, having a dance around your living-room…. anything that brings you some level of happiness and contentment. (Please note however, that these activities should be "safe activities" which do not intoxicate your mind or body. I do not recommend the consumption of drugs or alcohol.)

- **Phase 3: The Change**

As mentioned previously, whilst there are some people that experience an instantaneous healing, many people that experience emotional healing over time often find it difficult to pinpoint exactly when a change in their perception takes place. Jasmine's story at the beginning of this chapter illustrates this point. She says that she doesn't know exactly when or how the change occurred, but over time she had changed and experienced a healing.

There does come a time in one's journey when they recognise that their perception has changed. Sometimes the change can be quite significant, where the person realises that they no longer feel comfortable in their usual environment. I have worked with many people who change and then find themselves not fitting in with their usual friends circle. The person begins to think and behave differently, and starts to live life through a renewed perception.

Do not however be mistaken: life does not become obstacle-free. Individuals still experience life's obstacles; they still have families and jobs in which they need to remain integrated, but their approach to these challenges is different. It is also important to realise that change is on going and a person continues to experience shifts in consciousness over time. It is very possible that you could read the same personal development book over ten years, and each time you read it, you learn something new from it. The information in the book has remained the same, but your perception and understanding has changed and therefore you are able to interpret the information differently.

• Phase 4: Living the Change

Phase 4 is about continuing the combination of *doing* and *being,* as emotional wellbeing requires some effort on our part. People leave therapy with tools, techniques and hopefully a higher level of awareness; but life still happens, and if we're not mindful, old thoughts and behaviours may arise once again. It is important to remember that we become what we think about the most. Yes, it is important to acknowledge negative feelings when they arise but it is equally important to recognise that these feelings will pass. It is also necessary to engage in positive books, movies, audios and good company to keep yourself focused on positivity. The next chapter will discuss tools for emotional healing in more detail.

Element 2 Summary

- There are two types of healing: *specific* healing, which deals with specific issues; and *deeper* healing which is a deep shift in perception. When combined. Both types of healing work on the person as a 'whole'.

- Healing does not necessarily occur in a linear fashion and is quite often a case of two steps forward and one step backwards.

- Emotional healing occurs in its own time and is not a process that can be forced.

- Healing is a combination of *intention* and *allowing*. We use our intention to initiate healing but there does come a point when we need to *allow* the process to occur.

8
The Third Element:
Tools for Healing

This element highlights some tools that we can use to propel the Transcendent Healing Process.

Tool #1: Be Ready, Willing and Committed

Most people think that they are ready, willing and committed to changing, but are they really? Being ready, willing and committed means that you will have to put in constant work, as real change takes dedication and patience. It means that we have to be aware of our thoughts and actions on a frequent basis; it also means that we have to be willing to go deep and question the validity of our strongest beliefs.

Deep change requires that we observe, question, strip away our masks and look at ourselves for who we really are. This is a process that requires us to be ok with vulnerability as it may be the first time that we are really exploring our innermost thoughts, feelings, actions and fears. Quite simply, it may be the first time that we are getting to know ourselves – and it may be uncomfortable in parts.

It is also worth remembering that the journey of deeper healing will most likely be a life-long occurrence. I tell my clients that their journey does not stop with the end of therapy, but rather continues as they begin to experience life through a renewed perception. I tell them that they will still face challenging situations, thoughts and feelings, but their task is to continually remember who they really are. I ask them to remember what they need to do in order to take care of themselves physically and emotionally; and most important of all, I ask them to continue exploring and engaging in activities that will continue to propel them forward.

Tool #2: Work on Changing Perception

We experience life according to our perceptions; hence a change in perception equals a change in the way in which we experience life. In chapter six I mentioned that *not recognising our true purpose and true identities as souls is what creates an emotionally wounded heart,* hence correcting perception is about gradually coming closer to expressing the truth about who we really are – magnificent individuals with huge potential.

Right from childhood, my brother Aman had always been a sociable character - the kind of person that would brighten up any atmosphere just by being present. He was popular in school and university, and had a good group of loyal friends. A few years back he graduated from university with a good degree in business and marketing, and fortunately a family member had helped line up an interview with a good electronics firm. Aman was excited about entering the working world and was confident that he would perform well in the interview.

The day of the interview arrived and I remember Aman stepping outside to take the call in the garden. (The interview involved several phases with the first being a telephone phase). After a while he came inside and I could tell straight away from the look on his face, that something wasn't right. He told me that the interview had gone really well, until he accidently made a mistake at the very end. He felt that he had ruined his chances of getting the job – and he was right. The next day he learned that he wasn't successful in his attempt, and as a result was left feeling quite depressed. He felt as if he had let the family down - especially since the interview was arranged by a family member. He was angry with himself for making the mistake that he did and felt completely disheartened. He also lost all confidence in his ability to pass an interview and get a good job.

A few weeks later I offered him a spare ticket to a motivational seminar that I was attending. I knew he wasn't really the type to attend seminars, so I was pleasantly surprised when he accepted the offer. As it happens, that seminar changed his perception completely. To this day he is not sure exactly how the change occurred, but by the evening of that day he had decided that he was good enough and smart enough to get a job. And he did – within a week. He has gone on to do tremendously well and has a natural gift for understanding human behaviour, which makes him an excellent sales person. In fact, he is one of the few people that I know that has mastered the interview process so well that he could get into another job within days if he needed to.

A change in perception allows us to experience the bigger picture. It gifts us the opportunity to see not only the magnificence in ourselves, but also in others. A change in perception also transforms fear into courage and allows us to become comfortable stepping into the unknown, as we begin to recognise that we cannot control everything. We realise that the greatest, most mind-blowing, knock-your-socks off-type-of-experience occurs when we least expect it, in an unexplained way that we could never have foreseen. A change in perception allows the Transcendent part of us to inspire the greatest of action within us.

In the last chapter I explained that some of my clients still continue to come in for occasional sessions even once their specific issues had healed. They no longer required therapy for anything in particular, but rather they could feel themselves experiencing a shift in perception through the information that we explored during these sessions. A shift in perception can come about in many ways and within any time frame. Sometimes the change occurs randomly without any conscious input from ourselves, whereas at other times *we* actively work on changing our perception. So what does it take to experience a shift in perception?

Fundamentally, the shift comes about when we experience a change in our belief system, which enables us to view things from a different perspective. Therapy is one way in which the shift occurs. As individuals begin to talk through their issues and observe their thoughts and behaviours, they begin to see things from a different perspective and this reflection often brings about a change. In order to bring about an even deeper shift we can begin to question the grander spiritual purpose of life: who are we, where have we come from and where will we go once we die? We can look to those who have been here before us and also those who have experienced near-death states or miraculous healing. I find that reading about real life miracles is a powerful perception-changer because for a short period of time it takes us away for our daily routine life, which for many people can look the same: wake-up, freshen-up, breakfast, work, lunch, work again, come home, cook, do the chores, spend time with the family and then go to sleep. We get so involved in our routines that we forget to look outside of ourselves and therefore miss some of the beautiful things that go on around us. We become accustomed to reading the daily news that reports all that is not well with the world, and we watch dramas in which character egos create the storyline. Not that there is anything wrong with either of these, and indeed the news can be very useful in highlighting how we desperately need to implement personal and global change; but if we are not careful, then taking these steps repetitively fuels a belief system that isn't serving us too well. Now more than ever, we need to believe that things can be different. We need to understand that we are not merely individuals to which things happen, but rather we have the power to make things happen. Although we cannot control all outcomes, we can make a choice to live life differently: to eat healthily, to exercise regularly, to love and laugh frequently, and to look for miracles that remind us of our magnificence.

Watching, reading or spending time with people that inspire us will create a change in perception. If you're looking to achieve something in particular then look for ways in which it can be done, as opposed to finding ways in which it cannot be done. Look to the people who have achieved their dreams against all the odds and you will realise that there is a common theme: the way in which they think and the way in which they view things. It is worth noting that some of the most successful people have come from the most humble beginnings.

Service is another way in which we are able to change perception. Making a difference in someone's life, no matter how small can help to shift our perception. Serving someone (from a place of love and not obligation) not only helps them but also helps us, because on some level it makes us feel good and it connects us as human beings. Although natural disasters can be detrimental to both individuals and communities, they also bring about a heightened show of compassion. When a severe natural disaster occurs, it strips away our egos and brings forth love, compassion and kindness. We begin to see people from all walks of life coming together to help one another. In the midst of disaster we suddenly recognise that there is no amount of money, status or material belongings that can save us. Ultimately, apart from the surface appearance, there is nothing that differentiates us from one another. At the end of it, we are all people that experience love and pain, and none of us can escape the fact that one day we will leave these physical bodies. We all have the same basic needs and at the end of our lives the only thing that will really count is *have we used our life to make a difference?* How much have we loved? How kind have we been? How much compassion have we shown? Have we lived authentically? And have we played our part in leaving a better world for our future generations?

Changing perception is about recognising that every situation can be viewed in a both a positive and a negative way. Every experience, no matter how challenging offers us the opportunity of personal growth and gives us a choice of how we wish to respond. In any given moment and circumstance we can choose forgiveness over revenge, kindness over hostility, and love over hate. It is perception that allows us to transform the darkest times in our lives into the greatest gifts that we can offer. This is why we sometimes find people who have recovered from a particular ailment will go on to help others who are experiencing the same challenge. It is important to realise that perception is a choice: a choice that can create the experience of inner peace or inner suffering.

Tool #3: Observe Your Stories and Question Your Beliefs

Another great tool to aid emotional healing is to observe your stories and question your beliefs. What many of us don't realise is that, we are engaged in an internal dialogue most of the time. We are constantly interpreting situations and telling ourselves stories based about what we perceive. If we wish to experience a state of inner joy, then we must observe the stories that we tell ourselves and question their validity. We must take a thorough look at our beliefs and ask ourselves whether these beliefs are serving us in the correct manner. Here are some strategies that will help you to observe your inner dialogue:

1) *Be objective.* Sometimes we can get so caught up in our thoughts that we don't see the situation clearly. For a few moments, imagine that you are an outsider looking in on the challenge. I often ask clients to imagine that they are watching a movie of the situation with actors playing out the roles. I ask them to consider each actor's feelings,

and also the reasoning behind their actions. This exercise allows the client to practice objectivity and empathy – it allows them to step into someone else's shoes and try and understand their point of view, and also to see whether they, themselves are perceiving the situation accurately. Based on this, I ask them to reflect upon their internal dialogue. What have they been telling themselves about the situation? And most importantly, is it true – have they perceived the situation accurately?

When Anna was 18, she came to see me about her relationship with food. Anna was aware that she was developing an unhealthy attitude towards food and eating, and wanted to understand how she could stop this from progressing. Although she was considered to be a healthy weight and size for her age, she still felt fat. We soon discovered that Anna had been comparing herself to some of the models in the magazines that she had been reading. This had created a negative inner dialogue within her, where she frequently told her self that she wasn't good enough and that she had to eat less to be thinner.

During sessions, I asked Anna to question her inner dialogue. I asked her to look at the truth of the situation - to view the situation *as it was*, not as she *thought* it was. We also explored how images were sometimes photoshopped in magazines and how this changed the way that someone looked. In time Anna began to realise the importance of observing and questioning her thoughts. She understood that although her mind was immensely useful, it wasn't always accurate in the way that it perceived situations, and hence at times she needed to step back, observe her thoughts, and question their validity.

2) *Spend some time daily, in silence, observing your thoughts.* Perhaps one of the most useful features that we as Humans possess is the ability to observe our own thoughts. Consider this: there is a part of our mind that thinks the thought, but there is also a part of our mind that realises it is thinking the thought. Anyone who has had experience breaking free from an addiction will know that, at times the mind can be very convincing in its quest to take us back to the negative behaviour.

However, part of breaking free is recognising when the mind is doing this and then choosing not to engage in the addiction.

I have worked with many people in the past who have gotten into the habit of reacting instantly to a situation. They become so involved in both the incident and their internal dialogue, that they don't stop to think about their response, or whether they are perceiving the situation accurately. This quite often results in further arguing, anger and resentment.

When we take some time out daily to sit in silence, breathe, relax and observe our thoughts, we open the door to awareness. Observing our thoughts means that we watch what is going on in our mind without any judgement. As we do this we become aware of what we really think about on a daily basis, and we recognise how many of these thoughts are not conducive to our wellbeing.

The more we practice observing our thoughts, the more we allow *awareness* into our experience; and it is awareness that shifts our perspective. As we start to question our actions and responses, we become better equipped to deal with challenging situations.

3) *What role are you playing?* Along with Dr. Eric Berne, a number of other people in the field of Psychology have talked about the different facets of our personalities: *the child, the parent and the adult.* These are three different types of internal dialogues that take place within us.

The child is the part of us that seeks instant gratification. A child does not have adequate knowledge to make informed decisions, and hence when it wants something, it goes for it without considering the consequences. When *the child* aspect plays out in us, it takes action without having any regard for the consequence. It is the part of us that spends money when we know we can't really afford to, or indulges in sweet treats when we know that it will have an adverse effect on our health.

The *Parent* aspect within us is our authoritarian voice and is highly moralistic. This conditioning comes from childhood and is taught to us by the adults around us. As we grow older we experience this as the voice within which tells us what we *should* and *should not* do. For example, our internal adult often speaks when we go on a diet and choose to indulge in a "forbidden" food. The adult will say things like, "how could you have eaten that?", or "how stupid of you to consume all of those extra calories." This parent aspect is our critical, judgmental voice.

The *Adult* is the rational aspect. This is the part of us that thinks about a situation and looks at the bigger picture before responding. It weighs up the pros and cons of a situation and then acts accordingly. If we want to have peaceful and rational encounters with both ourselves and other people then we need to work on developing this aspect of ourselves. *Stop-breathe-relax-think and act* is a useful sequence strategy to use. This strategy should not take more than a few minutes to implement:

1) *Stop:* Take a moment and stop what you are doing. You may want to distance yourself from the situation, so that you have some space to reflect.

2) *Breathe:* Before you take any action, just take some time to notice your breathing. Focus on each in-breath and each out-breath. The idea is not to force deep breathing, but rather to just become aware of how you are breathing. You may then choose to take a deeper breath to help you relax.

3) *Relax:* Focus on relaxing your muscles. Consciously relax all of the muscles in your head, pay special attention to your temple area and your jaw as we often tense these during stressful situations. Allow your shoulders to drop and relax, followed by your arms, chest abdomen, back, pelvic area, thighs, knees, calves, ankles, and feet.

4) *Think:* Now that you have re-centred yourself, spend some time thinking about your next action. Think about the consequences that your action will produce and ask yourself if this is an experience that you wish to manifest.

5) *Act:* Once you have thought about your action, take the step and act.

It is also worth remembering that both the child and parent personalities can be irrational in thought, and usually co-exist. Let's look at the diet example again; let us assume that we are eating healthily to maintain good health. However, whilst out in a restaurant one day, our child aspect comes into play and we choose a very indulgent dish followed by a rich dessert. At this point, both the adult and the parent aspects are silent. Instead the child is running the show. It is not thinking about the consequences, but rather about instant gratification. Once we have finished our meal, the adult aspect comes in and criticizes our actions - creating a conflict within. If we would have utilised our adult aspect then firstly, we probably would have made a different choice; and secondly, even if we chose to indulge, the adult would have moved past it and resumed healthy eating for the next meal again — without the critical parent coming into play. The adult response would be rational.

Start to observe and become aware of the different personality aspects that play out in you. The more you recognise these different aspects, the more you will be able to understand yourself and others. You will also find it easier to change your behaviour. Work on strengthening your adult aspect by using the strategy mentioned above.

Tool #4: Express Your Authenticity

Bella was a bright, ambitious young girl who had high aspirations of working in the field of finance. At the age of twenty-three years old she had secured herself an excellent position working in a city bank and was looking forward to climbing the corporate ladder. Bella was born into the Indian culture and her family followed the traditions strictly, expecting her to marry in her early twenties. Her parents had already found a suitable boy and arranged a date for the families to meet officially. Although she was allowed to get to know him first, it was expected that Bella would agree to the proposal. Not wanting to go against her culture or her family, Bella agreed and the couple were married within the following year.

Although Bella's parents were happy to let her study and work, her in-laws took a slightly different stance. They were well natured and treated her well otherwise, but they followed a particularly traditional belief system. They requested that she leave her job and manage the household duties instead, saying that the family was not short of money and that she did not need to work outside. Rather, she was expected to stay at home and cook, clean, feed the family, and of course have children soon enough.

Although Bella tried to protest, she knew that she would have to give-in if she wanted her marriage to work. She knew how difficult it would be for her parents if this union failed to work, and hence she decided to embrace her new life.

Over the years Bella continued not to express her authenticity. She was very well respected in the family, fulfilled her duties well and, in the eyes of society had a successful marriage. But inside Bella was empty and deep down she felt resentment about her situation. Over time, this manifested as overeating, anger and irritation. The once bright and ambitious young girl didn't even recognise who she was at times.

Once her children had left home, Bella found herself feeling deeply unhappy. Although she still had her husband and in-laws at home, she felt as lonely and without purpose. She had spent so much time looking after other people that she had forgotten to nourish herself both physically and emotionally in the process. It was at this point that Bella decided to come in for therapy. She soon recognised that she had to reconnect with herself again in order to experience happiness, and so she started off by taking out time for herself to do the small things that she really enjoyed. At first the family weren't pleased with this change because it meant that their normal routine was being disturbed. However, after some time, Bella's husband started to see the positive impact that these steps were having on her, and began to understand and accept the change.

The dictionary definition of authenticity includes the words: *authorship, genuine* and *origin*. Therefore to be authentic is to express who you *genuinely* are. It means to live your truth and to be the author of your life. Authenticity is a gift that we all have been born with. We are all unique in our own way and we all have something special to contribute to humanity. Authenticity is what comes to us naturally; 'fitting-in' is what we learn to do.

One of the main challenges that we face with authenticity is that, as children we are not encouraged to follow our hearts and be ourselves. From a young age we learn about the roles that we are expected to play and quite often we do not question these. We look around us and find that others seem to be doing the same thing too; hence we study I.T instead of music, we take a job in a bank instead of pursuing art and we choose to do what is practical over what inherently feels right. Now, obviously there is nothing wrong with studying I.T, working in a bank if that is really what you want to do; but when we follow a path that that we know is not our internal calling, we cease to express our authenticity and starve ourselves of a form of joy that we have been born to experience. We become accustomed to wearing masks and hiding who we truly are, and sometimes we do this for so long that we completely lose connection with ourselves.

Done in the right way, authentic living is an internal process. It asks us to be aware of our thoughts and feelings and enables us to have more compassion and understanding for others. We come to accept others for who they are and allow them to just 'be.' Authenticity is not about being entirely selfish or inconsiderate. You may have had encounters in the past with people who consider themselves to be authentic. They come across as being very direct and speak the truth as they see it. However, the encounter is not an uplifting experience and instead may leave you feeling hurt or not so good about yourself. It is necessary to recognise that whilst speaking your truth is important, so are other people's feelings. If we were to teach children how to live authentically, we would not teach it as a stand-alone topic, but rather we would teach it alongside kindness, compassion, empathy and understanding. This means that the child will learn how to follow their hearts as well as being considerate towards others. They learn how to achieve a balance between self-love and love for others.

We need to be especially mindful about this when we make the transition from living a non-authentic life to more of an authentic life. When someone spends a significant amount of their life living non-authentically, they become emotionally wounded, and will most likely harbour negative emotions. Then, when they begin to speak their truth, they may end up taking on a *completely* carefree attitude where they say and do whatever they want with no consideration about the impact of their actions on others. Therefore, it is important to remember that authenticity is not about the other person and their actions, but rather about understanding yourself and why you respond in certain ways. Here are some ways in which you can begin to connect with your authenticity:

1) *Ask Yourself Who You Really Are*

Spend some time reflecting upon who you *really* are. What are your core values and beliefs and are they congruent with your actions? For example, let's say you think that you are a good natured, patient and compassionate person. Now, step back for a moment and reflect upon your behaviour. How do you treat others around you? What do your personal relationships look like? Sometimes it can help to close your eyes and imagine that you are watching a movie of your interactions with people. This will give you an outsider's perspective on actions, and you get to observe your behaviour objectively.

Reflect upon the different areas of your life such as work, health, family and leisure time. How authentic is your expression in these areas? Is your work fulfilling, or do you feel that you are here to do something else? Do you eat unhealthily even though deep down you feel that you should be taking better care of yourself? And how well do you relate to your family? Also, do you take time out to do things that nourish you on every level – when was the last time you engaged in a hobby that you really enjoyed?

As you begin to express your authenticity, be mindful about those around you. There may be family members, friends, colleagues and acquaintances that will find your change difficult to handle. Think carefully about how you communicate with them and try to come from a place of love as you begin to be more 'you'.

2) *Become More Self-aware*

Start to observe your behaviour frequently and pay attention to when you act non-authentically. Each time you recognise that you are behaving in such a manner, realise that it is an opportunity for you to learn more about yourself. In a very non-judgemental, gentle manner, ask yourself: in what way is wearing a mask serving you? Why do feel the need to perhaps eat unhealthily, or not express your opinion fully? At the same time remind yourself that you are part of a Transcendent Mind and that you have just as much right as anyone else to be yourself, for you are way more magnificent than what you realise.

Also it is important to realise that your expression of authenticity will change as you learn more about yourself. The more you connect with your deepest feelings and the more you understand about yourself, the more authenticity you will express. Consider this: authenticity comes from expressing our truth, and our truth is *who we really are.* Therefore this expression will be deeply connected to the Transcendent Mind, and because this is the case, real authenticity will come from the heart. It will come from a place of joy and it will bring with it a sense of freedom, empathy and compassion – not just for ourselves but for others too. We will no longer live in a state of fear of upsetting others and at the same time, we will encourage others to live in a similar fashion. Life becomes a happier, richer and a deeply fulfilling experience.

3) *Accept Yourself Fully*

Accepting yourself means being ok with both your strengths and yourweaknesses. We are all human and we have all made mistakes, but to express our authenticity we have to be ok with ourselves, which means that we have to begin accepting ourselves. Forgive yourself for the mistakes that you have made in the past and start anew in this moment. Forgiveness does not mean that you ignore these past experiences, but rather that you look at them, learn from them and embrace them as part of your life experience. These experiences have made you who you are today and if you view them with positive perception, you can use them to help others. So work on accepting yourself fully because nobody here has ever lived a mistake-free life.

4) *Follow Your Intuition*

We know that our individual conscious minds cannot know everything or control every situation, and we also know that we are part of the Transcendent Mind. Our intuition is guidance from the Transcendent Mind and is the part of us that communicates information (quite often in a subtle way) to us when we need it. Therefore, pay attention to your gut feelings and begin to honour them. Ask yourself how you feel about certain people and situations, and begin to express yourself in a way that is coherent with your core values.

5) *Be Prepared*

Be prepared to feel vulnerable. Living authentically means that we are exploring and expressing our deepest feelings and this may make us feel vulnerable at times. It takes courage to be both open about how we are really feeling, and then communicating these feelings to others – especially if we are new to expressing this side of us. We will go through a process of observing and understand not just our own feelings, but also how others respond to our new expression.

It is worth remembering that there is a possibility that we will upset people around us as we begin to change. In the earlier example that I shared, Bella found that initially her family were not pleased with the way that she was changing. By Bella taking time out for herself, it meant that she had to cut back on her other 'duties' which of course had an impact on her immediate family as they had to start managing things for themselves. However, Bella gently explained to her husband that she needed some time out for herself so that she could feel better about herself and life again.

However, there may be times when no matter how gentle you are, and how effectively you try to communicate your change with the people closest to you, they still may not understand. They may not accept your change and they may judge your expression of authenticity. If this is the case then we have to allow them to be. It is about recognising that we are responsible for our thoughts and actions, but we cannot control what others think. Also, it is worth remembering that sometimes when others judge us for expressing our authenticity, it is because they have not yet learned how to express theirs.

Tool #5: Learn How to Relax

Learning how to relax is one of the most powerful tools that I have ever come across. Emotional suffering comes from overthinking issues, and quite often we become so busy thinking, that we fall deeper and deeper into the issues that are causing us stress. We become entangled in the circumstance - completely engulfed in the story. Stress also plays a major role in our physical health, affecting for example, our weight, cholesterol and digestive systems.

Relaxation creates 'space' in our mind. It forms an internal environment within us that allows us to think more rationally. We are able to step outside of the issue and think about our next step. Perhaps the most important factor to remember about emotional wellbeing is this: *you cannot be stressed and relaxed at the same time.* This is a profound statement because it means that no matter what you are experiencing, if you can take the time out and train yourself to relax, then in any given moment you can exercise a choice: do I want to experience stress or do I want to experience relaxation?

There are a few dictionary definitions for relaxation, but the one I like best is this: *relaxation is a state where you are free from tension and anxiety.* Different people relax in different ways. Some people find that watching television or having a hot soak in the bath helps them to unwind after a long day. There are also many people that find going to the gym is a very useful way to help release stress and tension. The point of relaxation is to relax your body as well as your mind. Here are some things for you to consider, **but please remember do these exercises in a safe place and do not practice whilst driving or operating machinery**:

1) *Take some time out for deep breathing daily.* Taking a few short deep-breathing breaks can make a significant difference in your day. Make sure you're sitting comfortably with your back straight, and place one hand on your stomach. Breathe in slowly, steadily and deeply through your nose. As you do this you should feel the hand on your stomach extending outwards. (This is an indication that you are breathing deeply into your stomach). Hold for a few seconds. (Only hold your

breath for a length of time that is comfortable for you.) When you're ready, exhale through your mouth slowly and steadily. As you exhale you should feel your stomach coming back its normal position. Wait a few seconds and repeat the process again. It may be a good idea to pace these breathing cycles out, as too many of them too close together can cause you to become dizzy.

2) *Use the stop-breath-relax strategy often.* In Tool #3, I outlined a process where you relax all of the muscles in your body. This is a very useful exercise to help relieve tension. (In fact, quite often people do not realise that they are holding tension until they actively relax their muscles.)

 Once again ensure that you are sitting comfortably in a safe and preferably quiet environment. Draw your attention to, and become aware of your breathing to begin the relaxation process. You may wish to close your eyes. Consciously begin to relax all of the muscles in your head, pay special attention to your temple area and your jaw as we often hold a lot of tension here. Allow your shoulders to drop and relax, followed by your arms, chest abdomen, back, pelvic area, thighs, knees, calves, ankles, and feet. Feel the feeling of relaxation moving right down to the tips of your toes.

 Spend a few moments just enjoying the feeling of your body being relaxed, and if you find yourself thinking a stressful thought, draw your attention back to your breathing.

3) *Relaxation and feeling.* One of the most common things that clients tell me is that they cannot stop thinking. This exercise is a great tool that helps quieten the mind. Ensure that you are sitting comfortably in a safe and preferably quiet environment. Draw your attention to, and become aware of your breathing to begin the relaxation process. You may wish to close your eyes. Consciously begin to relax all of the muscles in your head, pay special attention to your temple area and your jaw as we often hold a lot of tension here. Allow your shoulders to drop and relax, followed by your arms, chest abdomen, back, pelvic area, thighs,

knees, calves, ankles, and feet. Feel the feeling of relaxation moving right down to the tips of your toes.

Now that your body should be feeling more relaxed, draw all of your attention into your right foot. What can you *feel inside* of your foot? Some people misinterpret this question and will say things like; 'I can feel my foot inside my shoe.' However, I am asking that you go *inside of your foot*. What can you feel? Does your foot feel hot, or cold? Can you feel a pulsating or a tingling feeling? Does you foot feel heavy or light? Keep all of your attention here and engage in the *feeling*. Do this exercise for a couple of minutes or more and you will find that your incessant thinking will have ceased for that short period of time.

4) *Engage in activities that help you to relax.* Aside from the breathing and muscle exercise that I have outlined above, it is important that you take the time out to engage in activities that help you to relax. Perhaps think about going to the gym, taking a yoga or meditation class. There are plenty of good books and audios that will help you learn more about meditation and relaxation. Remember the key: you can not be in a state of stress and relaxation at the same time, so the more that you make the conscious effort to relax-on-demand, the better you will be able to manage stress.

Please also remember to ensure that you are relaxing in a healthy manner. For example, I do not recommend that you use alcohol or any other intoxicating substance to achieve relaxation, but rather use the exercises that I have outlined above as a starting point, and then explore their different variations.

Tool #6: Acceptance

This was the fourth time that Andy had to move house in three years. Tired of having to pack and uproot himself again, Andy could feel that the frustration was beginning to build. Still living at home with his family – which he considered to be rather dysfunctional, he felt angry at the way in which life had presented him with challenging circumstances. Not knowing how to handle the shift, Andy became angry, distant and snappy with those around him. Andy was stuck once again with the challenge of 'change' - something that he did not like.

Change is something that is certain to occur. It does not matter how much we attempt to plan our lives, or risk-assess for potential obstacles, life has a way of gaining, what we perceive to be, the upper hand. When such situations occur, *acceptance* becomes our greatest aid. It is a tool that helps to minimise our emotional suffering. Acceptance is the willingness to tolerate a situation. It is about understanding that sometimes there is nothing that we can do about a particular occurrence, and if we choose to hold on to the negative perception that we have formed about it, we will experience emotional and physiological suffering.

Acceptance is also a very useful concept to apply to other people as well. We need to accept that we cannot change another, and that we need to let people *be*. At the very core we're all connected via the Transcendent Mind, we are the same — we operate in the same way; but years and layers of emotional wounding cause us to behave differently. If we accepted people as they were and if we became tolerant of one another's differences, the world would be a better place. Here, it is important to recognise that I am not just referring to accepting groups of people that are different to us, such as those of another faith or country; but rather I am also talking about accepting our nearest and dearest — those people who are closest to us. We can at times have expectations of family members and friends, but we must remember that they are here to fulfil their calling too, and this of course may look very different to the expectations that we have of them. For example, I have met people who expect their children to follow a particular career path, marry a partner that has been chosen for them or dress and behave in a particular way. The children however have their own personalities, dreams and aspirations, and in many cases the parents experience much emotional suffering before they decide to implement acceptance.

There are however a few things to consider. Although acceptance is an extremely useful tool, we need to exercise a level of discernment when we apply it. Acceptance does not mean that we drop our values and boundaries, as there may be situations that require us to put forward our point and to stand up for what we believe in. Certain groups of people throughout history have had to fight for positive change — women's voting rights being one such example. If these people simply accepted the way that things were, positive change might not have come about.

Physical abuse in a relationship would be another example where acceptance of the action would not be appropriate. Yes, it is a possibility that the individual on the receiving end of the abuse may have to accept that their partner is not changing, and hence the time to end the relationship may have come. Therefore we need to be mindful about where we apply acceptance.

To summarise, acceptance is about recognising that we cannot change or control another person. Acceptance is also about realising that we cannot control life all the time. Unexpected things happen, and at these times acceptance may be the only tool that will help us to reduce our emotional suffering.

Tool #7: Forgiveness

This tool begins with illustrating the power of forgiveness. The following story has been written by Tom Hudgens and is taken with permission from www.soulscode.com. [1]

Thirty years ago a man named John Black* raped and murdered my sister. In May, I visited him in prison and told him that I forgave him. The realization that I could actually do such a thing came unbidden. It wasn't something I struggled to attain. I just looked one day and there it was: my own voice saying, 'You can forgive him.' That voice spoke to me often. Eventually, I acted upon it.

Three years ago after a miserable year in a career that I loved in theory but not in practice, I was struck with the idea of attending a meditation retreat. I typed 'silent meditation retreat' into a search engine, and discovered Spirit Rock Meditation Centre, located on 400 acres in Marin County, California.

I hoped whomever Donald Rothberg was, he would be good.

I arrived excited and ready, and received the traditional insight meditation instructions: 'Sit quietly and comfortably, your spine erect, and follow the sensations of your breath…'

I was nine years old when my family received the news that my 22-year old sister was murdered. John Black, who was also 22, confessed. He received the death penalty, but the sentence was later commuted to life. Well into adulthood I wanted him dead, believing that, in this case, the death penalty was just.

A month after I attended that first retreat and began meditating, the realization came to me that I could forgive John Black. It was a quiet realization, arising with no fanfare.

About a year later, I attended a second, much larger retreat, presided by Sylvia Boorstein and Christopher Titmuss. During a Q A-type forum where people were checking in, I heard a powerful 'inquiry' – a woman bravely explained she was so beset with fear for her family in this unbalanced world that she was considering buying a gun.

I couldn't logically connect the notion of forgiving my sister's murderer with this woman's fear, but my realization became, in that moment, very, very insistent. Before, it had knocked on my door very quietly; now it was pounding.

A day or so later, my whole body was shaking, I inquired of Christopher Titmuss: 'Can I trust this realization to forgive? Does it mean I really need to do it?'

His reply was a cut-to-the-chase question: 'will you do it?'

'Oh yes,' I said.

If I could have just walked into that maximum-security prison, invisible, through the security fences, the tightly-coiled razor wire, past the guards, through the heavy, polished brass doors, through a succession of locked gates, up to the 'dorm' on Floor 6 and just sat down with John Black and talked with him, offering forgiveness, then turned around and invisibly walked out, I would have. But that wasn't possible.

I discovered a 'Victim-Offender Dialogue' program administered by the Texas Department of Criminal Justice. The program provides a structured, safe 'space' in which victims (or, in my case, close relatives of deceased victims) go to the prison and meet with offenders face-to-face, with a mediator present.

'Something we recommend' the young woman told me on the phone, 'is to write the offender a letter, telling him what you hope to get from the meeting.'

A month or two went by. Finally, I wrote:

Hello John. This may be hard to believe, but I come to you in a spirit of peace, compassion, and understanding. I loved my beautiful, dancing, dark-haired sister very much. I was 9-years-old when you took her from the world. Her sudden death, at your young hands, was deeply tragic and traumatic to the many of us who knew and loved her. We still remember her vividly and honor those memories . . . If you would like to know more about her, I will gladly tell you.

But I want you to know that I am willing to listen to whatever you wish to tell me. If you would like to tell me about your young life before the crime, I will listen. If you would like to talk about that night, February 27th, 1978, I will listen. If you would like to talk about 30 years in prison, I will listen.

Any questions you want to ask me, I will answer as completely and honestly as I am able. There is nothing specific that I need to hear from you: in meeting with you, I am not attached to any particular outcome. I'm doing this because this is the kind of world I want to live in, where people can come together and talk and come to deeper understandings . . . I wish you well, John.

Sincerely, Tom

April 27, 2007.

I wasn't assigned a mediator for almost a year. I knew very little about John Black. When I reached 22 years of age, some 17 years ago, I traveled to a courthouse in Austin, Texas, and read the transcript of the trial. Black's confession was blunt. I saw a picture of him — just an ordinary-looking, white guy with glasses. His signature was in grammar-school cursive. In the Texas penal system, the victim and/or family initiates the mediation/dialogue. But the offender has to agree to the process. It is entirely voluntary. He could back out at any time, as could I. Neither of us did.

'John Black is very eager for this meeting.' That was the short and simple email I received from Rick Warr, a mediator with the Texas Department of Criminal Justice who was arranging for me to meet John Black, the man serving a life sentence for raping and murdering my sister 30 years ago.

Why was he eager? I wondered. What did he think would happen? As the trip to Texas approached, I sought the wise counsel of Donald Rothberg, my first meditation teacher at Spirit Rock Meditation Center. He helped keep my thinking clear: 'All you know is that you have been given the opportunity to forgive him,' he told me. 'That's all you know. This is a big experiment.'

Rothberg's advice was essentially to 'practice' insight meditation — lots of it. Insight meditation is just sitting quietly, spine erect, eyes closed, concentrating on the physical sensation of the breath, and paying close attention to other physical sensations and thoughts as they arise, and pass away. We gradually come to recognize that our thoughts — including our fears and desires — are simply thoughts: Like all phenomena, they arise and pass away. We don't have to act on them, or even believe in them.

Normally, I meditate for a half-hour every morning, but to prepare for the journey, I began to meditate at least twice daily, and for longer periods. I also practiced 'loving kindness' meditation. This consists of mentally 'reciting' four traditional phrases, first directing them toward ourselves: 'May I be safe...may I be happy... may I be healthy...may I be at peace.' Following that, in the traditional sequence, the phrases are directed toward a benefactor, a dear friend, a 'neutral' person, then, finally, an 'enemy.'

Rothberg suggested that I direct the traditional meditative phrases of love toward myself, which I struggled with. I then remembered what another Spirit Rock teacher said: By truly loving ourselves, we create an ever more radiant, compassionate heart within us that can more readily embrace other people. In this way, paradoxically, loving and forgiving yourself is one of the kindest things you can do for others.

Several days before flying to Texas, I attended my third retreat. Most of the daytime sittings were outside, beneath Bay trees in a meadow in the hills above Spirit Rock. Nothing could have been more calming.

One morning, a truth struck me deeply — that all beings simply want to be happy, to thrive. Even a rapist-murderer, someone using, then taking, the life of another. In his deeply twisted confusion, in his unthinking, reactive, blind agony of desire and fear, even John Black wanted happiness.

The day before my visit, Warr visited me at my hotel and we spoke for two hours. A soft-spoken man in his 50s with a slight Texas accent, Warr carefully reviewed the questionnaires I had filled out. He asked if I wanted to see a photo of John Black. I did. Somehow it was very helpful: it calmed my expectations, narrowed the vast field of possibilities my mind was raking over and over, to see a photo of the man I'd meet the next day. His eyes had a particular intensity.

Warr told me that John Black often quoted Bible verses. He told me that John Black had 'college-graduate' intelligence. He told me that John Black was worried that I might take his habit of smiling as a sign of disrespect. He told me that John Black had written me a letter that he would read at the meeting.

That evening I was assailed by fear. I knew first to address the fear rationally — Warr had assured me that a prison is actually a very safe place. The fear took another form: that I might somehow flub the meeting. Donald Rothberg's words came back to me: 'All you know is *that you have been given the opportunity to forgive him.'*

In the weeks leading up to this moment, I had realized that, in the context of meditation and compassion and our interconnection as human beings, forgiving John Black was actually a very simple thing. I felt it, I knew it. Now all I needed to do was go to him and say it.

It took a half-hour to drive to Chesterson Unit, the prison in Huntsville, Texas that has housed my sister's killer, John Black,* for thirty years. Rick Warr, the mediator with the Criminal Justice department, picked me up at my hotel. We drove through the main entrance, past cornfields and cattle, and eventually reached the sprawling prison buildings, all made of yellow brick.

My meeting with Black — more than a year in the making, logistically, and many more than that, spiritually — was to take place at 10:00 a.m. We were taken to a stark, fluorescent-lit room used for officer trainings, where we waited for an endless 30 minutes. An inmate brought a tray with three pitchers — water, sweet iced tea, fruit punch. Eventually, in walked John Black, followed by a guard. In a flash, I recognized him from the grainy newspaper photos I had seen years ago: The same tall, thin frame, slightly stooped. He wore baggy, white elastic-waist pants, pajama-like, and loose pullover. His dark brown hair had a touch of gray. He wore thick glasses. He looked nervous.

I stood up and reached to shake his hand. 'Hello John,' I said. 'I'm Tom.' We sat across from each other at a folding table. Rick Warr sat at the head, between us. Black took out a letter. He apologized that it might be inadequate. He read in a soft voice with little intonation, in halting, staccato bursts. I leaned in just inches from his face to hear him:

> *Maybe it is best to simply be blunt and confess openly that I am guilty of the crime I am in prison for. Your sister was truly an innocent victim . . . I know that moment in time has forever affected and changed many lives, yours, your family's, my family's, my own . . . I cannot count the days*

*(months, years) I spent wishing and hoping and praying that
I could somehow go back and change what happened . . .
Difficult though reality may be, it is where we must live. My
crime against your sister was not something I had planned
. . . She was a total stranger to me and it was pure chance
that led our paths to cross that night. Her death was a tragic
mistake, a terrible crime . . . and yet, her death has become
the motivating factor behind the change in my life . . . I don't
mean the circumstances of where I now live, but in who I am
today as a human being.*

*Let me just profess my faith to you, Tom, as a
Christian. I believe wholeheartedly that Jesus died for the sins
of this world and that includes my sin against your sister . . .
It was in the County Jail, prior to my trial that the real horror
of my crime came home to me, and led me to fall down on my
knees seeking the Lord. It is because of your sister that I gave
my life to Christ, and now fully understand how very precious
and valuable life is.*

*I do believe [God] is ultimately in control of our
destiny and it is a fact that He works through people. Your
sister, even in death, is a part of this because she is a part of
who I have become. She remains a beacon, and helps to keep
me focused on the right path before me. She is a constant
reminder of the evil I have done, but she is also a very real
influence to do something positive with the life I have.*

*Tom, I don't know much about you, other than what
I glean from your letter, but you opened the door to this
communication and I hope it will not be closed once our
meeting has ended. I, too, desire to live in a world where
people can talk to one another. There was a time when I did
not know how to communicate . . . I think, through you, your
sister still has something yet to say to me. I can only pray that
through our meeting, God will somehow give you a peace and
sense of healing and comfort that can only come from Him .*

. . It is my hope that through (this meeting) . . . we will both be able to grow and learn and become better human beings. I know I have no right to expect it, but I do hope and pray that, maybe, one day, you might be able to find it in your heart to forgive me for what I have done.

Sincerely, John P. Black: #927B64; April 29, 2008

Toward the end, his eyes filled with tears, and he wiped them with his sleeve. My own eyes welled up, too. Now, it was my turn to talk. Not that long ago, I would never have believed that I would be here: Sitting face to face with John Black, the man who raped and killed my sister in 1978, chatting with him about his life. He apologized and asked for my forgiveness. And now it was time for me to put my lengthy spiritual preparation — which led me to this prison outside Huntsville, Texas — to practice.

I thanked John Black for reading his letter to me, for agreeing to meet, and asked him to be totally honest, even if he thought the truth might be painful or offensive. I told him that I was speaking on no one's behalf but my own, and that I was not trying to see if 'justice had been served.' Rather, I wanted to have open communication, compassion and understanding.

'Praise God,' John Black said simply and sincerely.

I then told him a story about the day I returned to my 3rd grade class after my sister's funeral. All my classmates were told what happened, but no one said anything to me, except a boy named Bobby who was deemed 'slower' than the rest of us; he had an especially sensitive and empathetic heart.

Bobby and I were talking on the playground. He was curious about the man who killed my sister. 'What color hair did he have?' he asked. Other, 'normal' children would have 'known enough' not to ask such a direct question. Not Bobby. I went home after school and asked my mother, and the next day I found Bobby. 'His hair is brown,' I told him.

Almost thirty years later, as the intention to forgive John Black arose, that story surfaced in my mind with new significance. The little-kid wisdom is this: We want to see the person who has done this. We want to bring him before us, to look at him.

John Black and I talked for two and a half hours, seated at our folding table, monitored by prison officials. I asked him about his early life. He described his family—his distant, truck-driving father, his brothers and his one sister. He ran track in high school. He didn't have stories of abuse or violence, yet he spoke of his deep insecurities. In his letter to me, Black wrote: 'I don't think it is possible in a letter or even in a meeting of several hours to recount all the things that defined who I was back in 1978, but I was definitely a lost soul, mentally sick and spiritually dead.' There wasn't, however, any particular incident or experience that illuminated the 'why' of the crime. It was to remain inexplicable.

John Black joined the military service at age 18, and wanted to be a policeman. He was married, unhappily, to a woman he had met in the military. We delved into the night of February 27, 1978, went through the events of the day, all the way through the crime and his arrest the following day. Neither of us flinched over the specifics.

I pressed him: 'What was going on in your mind at that point? What do you remember thinking?'

He tried to answer, but had explanation, saying, 'That's just it — I wasn't thinking.'

Learning to live with mystery is, to me, an important aspect of any spiritual path. How John Black, coming from a relatively stable home, with no prior criminal record nor any hard drug habit, with above-average intelligence, a wife and a job, could have done such a thing, will forever remain a troubling mystery.

John Black said he was grateful to have been arrested once he realized what he had done. His said his own actions were so incomprehensible that he wondered if he would have killed again had he not been caught. I had been told that John Black often quotes Bible verses, but he didn't do it much during our meeting. Nor did he smile a great deal, as I had been warned he would. In fact, there was a warmth about him, an intelligence, a spirit of inquiry in his eyes.

We took a short break, and when we resumed I told him about his victim, my spirited and beautiful sister. When you took my sister's life — I told the killer himself as we sat in a stark room in a Texas prison — there were, amazingly, seven people who considered her a best friend.

John Black, who is 30 years into a life sentence, had told me about his life, with the honesty I had asked for. Now I was telling him about his victim, who was taken from the world when she was 22 and I was just 9.

My sister, I told him, was a talented artist, proficient in many media: painting, drawing, lithography, photography, jewelry, sculpture. She was a straight-A student in the history of the art program at University of Texas, and the summer after she died, her friends mounted a show of her artwork at a gallery in Austin. I was her 'baby,' I told John Black — she gave me my first haircut, made all my early birthday cakes and made beautiful cards for every holiday. I told him how much I always looked forward to visiting her in Austin, how she would sit me on the tall stool of her drafting table with enormous sheets of drawing paper, pens and pencils and watercolors and markers galore. I told John Black how, when she'd come to tuck me in at night, she'd scratch my back until I'd fall asleep. My sister had a terrific, zany, silly sense of humor. After she died, I told John Black, we discovered cassette tapes of her singing-we never knew she could sing! On one, she accompanied herself on guitar, singing 'Angel of Montgomery,' but I accidentally taped over it. On another, she and two of her friends sang an old version of 'Rivers of Babylon.' The end of that song has a wonderful line:

So let the words of our mouths

And the meditations of our hearts

Be acceptable in thy sight

Over I

I told John Black our last memory of my sister. She had been visiting my mother and me, probably the Christmas/New Year's of 1977/78. She had arrived, as usual, by Greyhound bus, but on that visit my mother gave her our old car, a navy-blue Chevrolet Vega. This became our last image: My sister driving down our street in the Vega, while my mother and I stand on the curb, waving goodbye. As she drives off, she is waving gracefully out the window. We all keep waving until she turns the corner and is gone.

I asked John Black to describe his cell. He drew a small square on a piece of paper, and used a pen to point out his bed, a bookshelf, Bible, Concordance, other religious books, a calendar, a radio (he listens to a Christian station) and a fan. He is near a window, he said, so he can see animals outside. I ask him what he misses most about the outside world, the 'free world' as inmates call it. He told me that he misses living on his own schedule. Then he says he misses animals-he grew up in a rural area.

He is active in the prison chapel-he was chosen by the chaplain to be a deacon, and he even occasionally gives the sermon. He delivered his first sermon three years ago, the same year I began meditating at Spirit Rock in Marin County, California. The subject: reconciliation. I asked about opportunities he's had to help people. He struggled to answer this; the struggle, I believe, was to answer without pride. He then told me about an inmate who had killed many people and was being taunted by another inmate. The first inmate showed John Black a 'shank' that he intended to use to kill the guy taunting him. John Black talked him out of it, and got him to hand in the knife.

Finally, I took John Black's hands in mine. 'John,' I said. 'I forgive you for your crimes of raping and killing my sister. From what I can see today, you are a good, honest, intelligent, thoughtful man.' 'To me,' I went on, ''forgiveness' means I can accept what happened, that you did what you did, and that today, in this moment, I can wish you well, that I feel compassion towards you. And I hope that you can someday forgive yourself.'

'Praise God,' said John Black. 'Thank you. Thank you.'

At this point, the meeting was mostly over. Both John Black and I had to fill out one last brief questionnaire. As John Black was leaving the room, I did something that surprised us both: I put my arms around him. Though he held his hips at an angle, he returned the hug wholeheartedly, saying, 'Oh, I didn't know if this would be appropriate, but I hoped it would be.'

I looked down and saw his small leather-bound Bible, given to him 20 years ago.

'That sure looks well-worn,' I said.

'That,' he said, 'is my crutch.'

'Aww, no it's not,' I said, to which he replied: 'Oh, yes it is. It definitely is.'

We hear the term *'forgiveness'* often. It is something that we expect both ourselves and others to do, but rarely do we stop to ask ourselves what *forgiveness* means. Forgiveness is letting go of negative, bitter and resentful thoughts and feelings that we harbour against another. When we forgive someone we let go of the need for revenge and we make the decision to no longer hurt ourselves. You may have heard the phrase, *'hanging onto anger is like drinking poison and expecting the other person to die'*. Ill thoughts and feelings towards another person do not harm them, but rather, harm us on the inside because they create non-conducive physiological reactions in our body. They also create an emotional suffering that may for example, manifest as depression or anxiety. Therefore, to forgive someone is to release these negative thoughts and feelings, so that they are no longer causing you harm.

There are some people that I have worked with in the past who feel that by forgiving someone who has hurt them, they are saying that the hurtful behaviour is acceptable. This is not true. Forgiveness does not make hurtful behaviour acceptable, but rather is a tool for you to use to lessen or stop your own emotional suffering. We need to be able to make the distinction between the person who has hurt us and the action that they have taken. Firstly, we must recognise that we are all human beings and fundamentally we are all seeking the same thing: inner peace and happiness — even those people that inflict great pain and suffering are in search of inner contentment, and their actions somehow provide them with an instant, temporary happiness fix. These people still deserve our compassion. Remember that at the core we are all connected via the Transcendent Mind and we are all wired naturally with tendencies such as love, compassion, kindness and empathy. This is what connects us and this what creates transformations in consciousness.

When a person inflicts pain and suffering upon another, they are doing so from an emotionally wounded place because only *hurt people, hurt people*. They have forgotten who they really are and are no longer expressing their true natures. If we ourselves wish to reach a place of inner contentment, then we must try to look past our pain and understand the other person's suffering. Ask yourself what pain and suffering that person must have gone through in order to be able to inflict it upon somebody else? Where there is an infliction of pain, there is a lack of love and compassion. Remember that we cannot give another person what we do not have therefore, if we have experienced hurt and a lack of love and in the past; and if we have not been loved and nurtured in the right way, then our actions will come from a wounded place. (This is not to say that we blame our caregivers in anyway — because they too could only give us what they had. Our focus hence should not be on blame, but rather on healing our wounded aspects.)

As we begin to understand firstly, that we are all connected; and secondly the reasoning behind another's actions, then we open the door to developing compassion for them, and when we develop compassion, we are able to forgive. It does not matter *how much* we want to forgive someone, the willingness alone will not achieve it. Only true understanding and empathy will allow us to forgive, and through this we achieve emotional freedom.

Forgiveness does not mean that we accept the wrong actions of the person. In the example at the beginning of this section, John Black still remained in prison as a consequence of his actions. Tom Hudgens forgave John because he knew that it was something that he needed to do. Although challenging, Tom was able to separate the person from the action. Through a combination of meditating, reasoning, reflecting and accepting, Tom was able to make peace with John. In the process of it all, John Black too became a better person. He was aware of his actions and had experienced a change in perception.

Forgiveness is not about saying that the wrong action is acceptable, but rather it is about recognising that further hate, resentment and negative thought and action will not help the healing of either person. Forgiveness is about recognising that ultimately love is the most powerful healer. Yes, whilst a person does need to be responsible for their actions, they also need help to express their natural loving natures; for one who learns to love truly will naturally feel empathy and compassion for another, and will not engage in such harmful action.

Forgiveness and tolerance are signs of strength, not weakness. When we take the step to forgive someone, not only are we taking responsibility for own health and healing, but we are also acknowledging the Divine in others. Fundamentally, forgiveness is a tool to help us change our perception and come closer to expressing who we really are. Here are some key factors to remember about forgiveness:

1) *Forgiveness benefits you.* It is about finding peace within yourself and lessening your own emotional suffering. It is ok to feel negative emotions about the situation, and the likelihood is that you will feel negatively towards the person to begin with too. Allow the process to occur, but keep in mind that there is a difference between the person and action.

2) *Understand that there is a difference between the person and the action.* It is ok to have negative feelings about the action, but it is important to remember the fundamental, transcendent truth about the person. This may not be easy at first, but it is a very useful direction to start contemplating.

3) *Consider the following trio: empathy, compassion and forgiveness.* Empathy is the ability to understand another person's circumstances, feelings and motives. It is a powerful tool that we can use in the process of forgiveness because it allows us to gain a glimpse of why the person did what they did. Understanding

through empathy is what leads to compassion and compassion is what leads to forgiveness.

4) *Forgiveness may not necessarily mean reconciliation with the person.* If the person continues to behave in a negative manner, then it is perfectly ok (and safe) to distance yourself from them. Forgiving somebody is not about allowing them to continually hurt you, instead it is about firstly recognising what is going on within you; and secondly realising that the person's actions are coming from a wounded place. Both these factors will help you to find peace. Coming to this realisation does not mean that you have to integrate with them again and neither does it mean that they will change.

5) *Perhaps the most important thing to remember is that forgiveness may take time.* The process of empathy, compassion and forgiveness may not be a straight forward process – especially if the action has caused you immense pain, and the process may well be a case of taking two steps forward, followed by one step backwards. It may be an idea to talk to a trusted person or go for some counselling in order to work through the thoughts and feelings that you are experiencing. Remember that it took Tom Hudgens years whilst working with meditation before he could forgive John Black. In this case, John Black too went through a form of healing, however, not everyone's experience will look like this. In some cases, people do not achieve a connection with themselves and hence do not change.

6) *Remember to stay in the present moment.* Sometimes when we experience what we perceive to be a traumatic event, we can remain stuck there. Years may pass, but yet the pain may be as fresh as it was when we first experienced the event. It is important to remind yourself that each moment is a new moment, and an opportunity to experience life differently. The event may have occurred a while ago, but it is your current perception, thoughts

and feelings that are causing you the pain now. Using some relaxation techniques may help you to deal with the thoughts and feelings.

9

The Forth Element

The Role of Nutrition

*Before I begin to discuss this element, I do want to mention here that
I am not a qualified medical professional or nutritionist. The information
presented here should not be substituted for professional medical or
nutritional advice. The aim of this element is to highlight the role that
nutrition can play in emotional wellbeing.*

*

Deeper healing is all about approaching healing from a mind, body
and spirit perspective. Whilst we understand that we are part of a Transcendent
Mind, and that we need to release trapped energy, (which is the result of trauma
in the past); we also need to seriously consider the health of our physical
bodies.

Unless we begin to address healing from a mind, body and spirit
perspective, we will still continue to suffer in some way. We need to treat the
'whole' of ourselves, which means we need to address both the tangible and
the intangible parts of ourselves. Our body houses our spirit. It is the vehicle
through which we perceive human life and it is *essential* that we understand
how our body responds to nutrition and the environment. We are constantly
told that we need to eat our fruit and vegetables, but what we are not *explicitly*
told about is the effect that they have on our physical and emotional wellbeing.
We have given away our personal power where our nutritional needs are
concerned. Many of us do not even know what we are eating when we consume
a packaged food and similarly, we have no idea how our food is prepared and

packaged.

Our society is riddled with physical and emotional ailments that we focus on treating through conventional medicine. Many of us pay no serious attention to the part that we play in creating this toxic environment within us, and quite often we add to the toxicity through the medicine that we consume. I am not saying that conventional medicine is not important, because clearly in many cases it is life-saving. What I am saying is that we need to take full responsibility for our physical and emotional wellbeing, and this means that we need to address what we are feeding ourselves.

A combination of emotional issues as well as the physiological addictive nature of some foods can make it very difficult to eat in a way that nourishes the body. I have had an extremely troubled relationship with food in the past. I developed body image issues at quite a young age, and as soon as I was old enough, I joined my first official diet club. From around the age of fifteen up until my mid-twenties, (even-though my eating pattern was very erratic where I was either dieting or bingeing), I somehow managed to keep my weight in check. However, in my mid-twenties I could no longer continue this cycle, and in a short period of time I developed binge eating disorder. For almost six years, although I tried desperately to change, my eating remained severely out of control and I gained around seventy pounds of weight in the process.

After experiencing a major shake-up in my personal life, I finally hit rock bottom and knew that I had to do whatever it took to change. Gradually I found a way of managing the binge eating[11], but I still wasn't consuming the most nutritious food, and hence there was always somewhat of a chance that a relapse may occur.

A couple of years later I developed severe allergies and problems with my glands. On some days my glands would be so painful that I would be unable to turn my head properly. I had to take regular medication to keep the symptoms under control, and as one of the allergies were to grass and pollen, I was advised not to spend too much time in the outdoors in grassy areas. This was hard because I love the outdoors. Daily life was a constant struggle and I felt unwell most of the time.

---

11   If you want to learn more about how to break free from binge eating, then please refer to my earlier book *My Secret Affair with Chocolate Cake.*

One day, a friend of mine suggested that I should completely change my eating habits and move towards fresh juicing and a plant-based diet. I was unsure at first because I didn't know how I would cope without wheat and animal products, but out of desperation I took her advice.

I did lots of research on juicing beforehand and I knew that I had to be really careful because I had suffered with an eating disorder in the past. I started off on a Jason Vale programme and consumed nothing but freshly extracted juice for seven days. Admittedly, the first couple of days were challenging, but by day three I was starting to feel much better. I no longer suffered with headaches and lethargy. I was able to focus for longer periods of time and hence my work productivity significantly improved. Once my seven days were over, I transitioned into a plant-based diet, where I would still consume two or three juices a day and then have a healthy vegetarian meal in the evenings. The difference in my health was profound. As soon as I started juicing all the allergies disappeared - there were no more swollen faces and rashes on my skin, and within four weeks, my glands were functioning normally again. My blood tests were coming back normal and the doctor was surprised with the outcome.

I experienced such an improvement in my health that I decided to remain vegetarian. The juicing had reset my body to function normally again, so as I started introducing different food groups into my diet I was able to tell how my body responded to them. I realised that diary products caused me to experience flu-like symptoms and clouded my mental clarity, and hence I cut out most of these from my diet. I also noticed that I responded well to rice, but wheat would sometimes cause me to bloat. It took me a while to refine my diet, but eventually I got to a place where the food was working in harmony with my body.

Even though I had grown up hearing that good nutrition was important, I was still shocked to discover the impact that food had on my mind and body. I had previously suffered with binge eating disorder and when I removed certain foods, and certain combinations of foods, the binge eating tendencies disappeared. Yes, I would occasionally get a psychological craving for a food, and on occasions when I chose to eat that particular food, I realised that it did not taste as good as I thought it would. The *thought* of the food was much more appealing than the food itself.

Although this book is not about binge eating issues, I would like to mention that overeating or binge eating issues can be complex and different individuals experience the symptoms in different ways. For me, certain foods produced a strong physiological response to the extent where I felt out of control and driven to eat them. Addressing the psychology of food alone was not enough as these foods had an effect on my psychology. They had a 'drug-like' effect on me, and even today I know that if I choose to eat the way I used to, then my old symptoms will return once again.

Perhaps the most interesting revelation of all was the impact that the change in nutrition had on my emotional health. I was aware that nutrition was important to keep the mind and body functioning well, but I did not realise to what extent this was the case. I experienced a higher level of mental clarity as well as an improved mood state. The frequent headaches, which I had previously suffered with, disappeared completely, and I was able to concentrate for much longer periods. I was also much calmer in my mind and I no longer experienced incessant mind chatter. It felt as if there was 'space' in my mind that allowed me to think before responding.

Once I had personally experienced the benefits of nutrition, I started doing further research into the role that nutrition plays in emotional wellbeing. I soon learned that many people had experienced great benefits, both physical and emotional by changing their diets.

James Colquhoun and Laurentine ten Bosch, filmmakers behind *Food Matters* and *Hungry for Change* started their journey when James' father, Roy, was diagnosed with chronic fatigue syndrome[12]:

In 2003, James' father experienced a severe health crisis. After decades of working in stressful conditions and consuming a typical western diet, Roy Colquhoun's body completely shut down. Bedridden for months with depression, chronic fatigue, anxiety and severe flu-like symptoms, Roy sought the best medical care available. Psychiatrists and medical specialists recommended a myriad of drugs that did nothing to alleviate Roy's physical ailments and that Roy asserts, actually worsened his mental condition.

"My life was a psychotic daze and spiralling downward out of control,"

---

12 If you would like to learn more about nutrition then I suggest you watch, *Food Matters* and *Hungry for Change*. You can learn more about James and Laurentine, and also find out more about the two films at www.foodmatters.tv

Roy recalls. " Ultimately, this led to my psychiatrist admitting me to a specialist psychiatric hospital for a period of thirty days. This hospitalization did not help at all and all that was achieved was a change in the ingredients of my cocktail of prescription medication…Feelings of hopelessness started to predominate my life. Suicide was becoming a frightening and very real option."

As a professional businessman with obstinate faith in conventional practices, Roy was initially very unreceptive when James and Laurentine encouraged him to read about natural health methods they were learning about. Roy explains his attitude at the time was, "If the best of the medical profession could not help me, how could my son and daughter-in-law with their nutrition and vitamin-based approach help?"

James and Laurentine understood that it would take powerful measures to shock Roy into kicking his dangerous pharmaceutical drug habit. After realizing that he wasn't reading the books that they sent him, the duo set off around the world interviewing experienced doctors, researchers, naturopaths and journalists. Their reasoning was that if Roy wouldn't read the books then maybe he would listen to these experts on DVD.

"They arrived on my doorstep and I was told that they were not leaving until I recovered," Roy remembers. Seeing the filmed footage of all these experts had its desired effect. "After five years on heavy doses of anti-depressants, anti-psychotics, anxiety medication and sleeping tablets, I started taking therapeutic doses of vitamins and minerals and within a week had withdrawn from all prescriptive medication." Also, with some not so gentle persuasion according to Roy, " I was ordered onto a ten day detox, eating only raw food and no alcohol and continuing on a special cleansing diet thereafter."

The results? Nothing short of spectacular. Roy suffered none of the serious drug withdrawal side-effects cautioned by the medical profession. Today he is disease free, drug-free, twenty kilograms lighter, running twice a week and enjoying a happy retirement.

"We are not suggesting that pharmaceutical drugs do not have their place, we're suggesting that our overburdened healthcare practitioners perhaps do not have the time to educate people about nutrition and healthy living," James points out. "Food Matters was created to help fill that void."

Experts such as charlotte Gerson explain that the human body is self-curative when it functions in good health. She is adamant that "a normal, healthy body cannot and will not develop cancer or any other illness for that matter." Conversely, when our innate healing systems become damaged by an un-natural diet and a toxic environment, disease manifests. Whilst drugs have their place in medical emergencies, chronic use merely masks the symptom of disease and impedes profound healing. [1]

Roy's story highlights the importance of nutrition in mental health. Addressing one's psychology becomes difficult whilst his or her mental health is affected by nutrition. When we are dealing with emotional healing where an individual is consuming poor nutrition, it becomes challenging to ascertain how much of the emotional issue is a result of the poor nutrition being consumed. Therefore, nutrition is one of the key factors that I address in my practice, and although I am not qualified to give nutritional advice, I do encourage people to watch films such as *Food Matters* and *Hungry for Change*. I also encourage clients to see a good holistic nutritionist too. Although nutrition is not responsible for all of a person's issues, it may play a significant role.

Another amazing example is that of Fiona Watson's, Fiona says:

I was lying in bed one night in July 2013 when I fell upon a documentary called "Fat, Sick and Nearly Dead." I remember thinking it was a ridiculous name for a documentary but you know what – I had been going through a miserable time and it completely described how I felt! Joe Cross' words resonated with me from beginning to end. It was like a light bulb switched on in my head – the next day I ordered a juicer.

I was suffering from debilitating back spasms and was taking 500mg dihydrocodeine, 2 tablets, 4 times a day just to be able to move. I was also on antidepressants long term, and I was using alcohol as an emotional crutch. Two weeks in to change of diet and I realized I hadn't taken a single thing.

I have worked with a number of clients now who have seen a significant decrease in their levels of anxiety since addressing their diet. Each person is different and hence his or her trigger foods are different too: Client A, a 30 year old female, suffered from severe anxiety to the point at which it was affecting her daily life. Other immediate family members had also suffered with the same issue too. Not wanting to take medication, she was willing to try alternative methods first. Within a few days of changing her diet, she recognised that rice triggered a change in her behaviour, and she noticed an immediate decrease in her anxiety levels when she cut the food out.

Client B noticed that sugar triggered angry feelings within her, specifically sweets and chocolate. She also noticed that her son responded in the same way to sugary foods, hence she now watches her sugar consumption very carefully.

Client C, a 42-year-old male discovered that fast food and certain meats triggered anxiety within him. He expressed that when he ate a vegetarian diet, he was calmer and he was able to control his anger and negative emotions to a greater degree.

Neil Martin, founder of *Natural Juice Junkie* has also experienced the benefits of nutrition first hand. He states:

Just before my 23rd birthday my dad died of cancer aged just 50. I'm not sure that I know the words to even begin to describe how much I love my dad: my father, my hero, my mentor, my friend. I nearly used the word "loved" then, but the feelings I have for my Dad will always be with me, even if his life on this earth has passed. Perhaps losing him at such a young age should have made me focus more on my own health, but it didn't. Instead, it had the opposite effect.

I suspect I could write several books about the impact my Dad has made on my life and the effects of losing him, but for now at least I will try to keep this fairly brief. It's funny; having lost weight and improved my health in the last few years, lots of people ask how I've achieved this, yet very few (if any) ask how I gained the weight in the first place. At the time my Dad died I was a newlywed, young, healthy 22 year old who went to the gym most days and felt fit enough to take on the world. Then my whole world simply broke. One of the cornerstones of my very existence was gone and I had no idea how to cope with it. I won't bore you with the full details, but let's just say that I thought that if I was nearly half way through my own life then I was going to live it. Unfortunately I was misguided with the lifestyle that followed, thinking that living the good life was drinking more, eating whatever I liked and not "wasting my time" in the gym.

More than 10 years later I looked in the mirror and saw an old fat guy looking back at me. This wasn't the good life the adverts for all the food and drink I'd been consuming had promised. I had the flash car, the fancy clothes, etc. but I sure as hell wasn't living a life that made the most of every precious day.

My Dad was my inspiration for so many things in my life, but most of all; he inspired me to be the best Dad I can be. When I saw that fat, sick guy in the mirror, I feared that my kids would lose me too young and I simply could not allow this to happen, so I took control of my own future and changed my lifestyle.

In September 2009 I went to see a Nutritional Therapist who gave me various advice on how to clean up my diet. This led me to start researching diet and nutrition and one of the books talked about juicing. When I read about the concept of juicing vegetables to increase the volume of nutrients I was consuming, it immediately made sense to me, so I ordered a juicer. The first juice program I followed was Jason Vale's 7lbs in 7 days. I have to admit that I was initially a little skeptical about the idea of living on nothing but juice for 7 days and was convinced I would spend the week feeling hungry. Most people I mentioned it to thought I was mad too. This was a long time before Fat, Sick and Nearly Dead or the high media coverage of juice detox. A few months after reading the book, I had a week where I was working from home so I decided to give it a go. From memory I think I lost about 10 pounds that week. I wasn't hungry at all and was really surprised to be bursting with energy. When I first started juicing, weight was literally falling off me, but the weight loss was just a small part of my story. Before I started my journey to rediscover my health, I was asthmatic and had various other health problems, including IBS. I'd had cameras put inside my body, I'd had biopsies, but there was no wonder pill to heal me.

Since starting my journey I've lost over 5 stone (over 75 pounds) in weight and no longer suffer from asthma or any of the other health issues that affected my life on a daily basis.

I am a regular person and there is nothing particularly different about me. I firmly believe that if I can regain my health, lose weight and reverse the aging process, so can millions of others. [2]

The Riordan Clinic based in Wichita, Kansas is a non-profit organisation which focuses on nutrition based health. Since its inception in 1975, the clinic has integrated lifestyle and nutrition to help individuals find the cause of their illness. Their mission has been to stimulate an epidemic of health.

One of the founders of the Riordan Clinic, Dr. Hugh D. Riordan, published the following article on overcoming depression:

Depression affects about 17 to 19 million American adults each year. It is possible to become depressed because of the lack of a sufficient amount of a single trace element. Did you know every medical textbook, at least up until a few years ago, indicated that one of the most common effects of inadequate vitamin C is depression. We very seldom go to a psychiatrist who measures our vitamin C level.

Many years ago, I had a lady who was a teacher and was profoundly depressed. She had three years of psychotherapy prior to coming to The Centre. She had profound fatigue and was barely able to function at all. Our testing revealed that she had no detectable vitamin C, so we gave her 500 milligrams of vitamin C a day – not very much by our standards.

In a couple of weeks she thought a miracle had occurred. No miracle had occurred. She was low on vitamin C and depression is a natural consequence of that. She had very good insurance. A psychotherapist could have seen her every week for two years and the insurance company would have paid the entire bill. Our bill was for two office calls and three vitamin C levels. The company would not pay because vitamin C had nothing to do with depression, according to their payment schedule. If you are depressed, vitamin C is worth considering.

In studies at two area health centres, 30% of new admissions with a diagnosis of depression had low plasma vitamin C levels. Actually, we did this study a number of years ago and found that if you took a hundred people who are depressed without checking their level and gave them all vitamin C, 30% would get better. Statistically, that would be below the placebo level. That is why it is important to separate out the 30% from the large group; so the people who are low in vitamin C will obviously respond more to the vitamin C than the people who are not.

Of course, man and woman do not live by vitamin C alone. It is possible to become depressed because of a lack of a sufficient amount of a single trace element. The following is from an audio tape of a person who had this problem:

"I was getting more depressed. I had two grand babies coming at the end of July and I didn't want to see them. That's rather odd for a grandmother. I knew I wasn't up to helping my children with their children. I knew I had to teach. We needed the income. I never got any sleep and I wasn't worrying about my students. I teach learning disabled students. I love my job. I just didn't feel up to it and I knew something was wrong. I tried hypnosis to no avail. I tried several psychiatrists. My response was the completely opposite of what the medication I was taking was supposed to do. One psychiatrist knew enough to send me to The Centre. This wasn't just light depression; it was the inability to cope with life, inability to enjoy the company of my family. We couldn't go to dinner because I was allergic to so many foods. The thing that changed my life was calling back The Centre and letting them know that I wasn't feeling any better. They decided to give me double the amount of liquid zinc. Dr. Riordan told me how to take it. Instead of having it in a whole load of water, I just had a smidgen of water. In two day's time, when I had double the zinc, my husband said he had a new wife and he wasn't sure he could cope with me. We even brought my daughter here, who is severely depressed and we

know she will get help. She has some of the same nutrient needs that I have but not the need for zinc. But we are all happy about the two grand babies. I have also been able to do better with my students."

There were several important points mentioned in that little piece. One point is to measure what's going on. If you give zinc to a 100 people who are depressed, 99 of them are not going to do much with it. In her case, zinc seemed to be her particular thing. It is very important to look at the individual biochemistry to see what is missing and what needs to be improved. Then you can do a great deal. She also indicated that she wasn't doing very well initially and that's why we have to follow-up, to see what's going on. Her initial zinc, we knew was very low and the initial amount we gave her was not sufficient to raise it to the level that she needed.

Keep in mind that zinc is involved in at least 100 enzyme systems in the brain alone. So, it's a very important trace mineral. Certainly not the only one, but one that is worthy of consideration when brain tissue function is not optimum.

Serotonin tends to improve mood and promote relaxation. If you're going to do a study on serotonin, you need to collect the urine for 24 hours. The lab will inform you that avocados, pineapple, eggplant, plums, walnuts and pregnancy are going to affect the serotonin level.

According to a study done in Great Britain, 80% of people with mood disorders noticed that food choices affected how they felt. The food you choose: avocado, bananas and some walnuts, should pick up your serotonin level and, thus, enhance how you feel if you are depressed.

Sugar and alcohol are considered "food stressors," according to a British study. In the same study, water, vegetables, fruit and fish were considered "food supporters." Actually, researchers said that water was number one for subjects wanting to improve how they felt. As we get older, one of the major problems is dehydration. When we are young, the ratio of water inside the cell to outside the cell is 1.2 to 1. There is more water inside the cell than there is outside. By the time we are 60, the ratio is 0.8 to 1. Even if you are drinking enough water, you are dehydrating all the time. So the goal is to drink sufficient water.

The incidence of depressive disorders varies throughout the world. Japan has the lowest incidence of depression, as does Korea – 2%. Taiwan has 3%, The USA has 7%, New Zealand has 11% and France has 16%. It would appear that the dietary choices may have something to do with whether or not they are depressed. Japanese and Koreans eat a lot of fish. The omega-3 fat in most fish manipulates the brain chemicals in ways that boost mood. You can of course measure fatty acids to see what levels you have. If the brain is not working well, feed it what it needs!

Most people don't appreciate that food has something to do with how they feel. In addition to general responses to various foods, adverse reactions to specific foods can lead to depression. The Centre uses the cytotoxic text to detect adverse food reactions. The test is useful for people who have brain fog or are not thinking well. The test is done by separating out the white cells and then mixing them with various food antigens. If the white blood cells are happy and healthy, that food is fine. If there's a kill off in white blood cells, then you have a positive cytotoxic test. Limiting cytotoxic foods can improve brain function.

Neurotransmitters are derived from amino acids, which can be measured in blood and urine. Abnormal amino acids can be corrected nutritionally which should improve neurotransmitter and brain function. Adequate amounts of fatty acid, which are in every cell membrane, can have a stabilizing effect on mood. The cells talk to each other through fatty acids in the membrane.

Inadequate thyroid function can lead to depression. One can measure a standard thyroid test, thyroid stimulating hormone (TSH), or thyroxine (T4). We measure triiodothyronine (T3), which is the active hormone that gets into the cell.

Hormonal changes, such as low testosterone, have been shown to affect depression. The same thing is true with female hormonal imbalances.

Short term depression in response to unpleasant life events is normal and does not necessarily need an anti depressant. In our culture right now, there is the notion that one should never feel depressed about anything. When certain things happen, you ought to feel depressed. If it is a short term thing, it usually doesn't need treatment.

People who are depressed have been shown to breathe less deeply than people who are not depressed. You can de-stress by deep breathing. Take five deep breaths and hold each one for six seconds. Do this four times a day. This decreases tension. You have two sides of the nervous system, the central nervous system and the autonomic nervous system. All day long we are tensing up with what is going on, and the autonomic nervous system tenses too. It is like tightening a ratchet. When you take five deep breaths, it is like releasing the ratchet.

Exercise has been shown to be useful in eliminating depression. There are studies at the University of Wisconsin that show that getting people who are depressed to run in groups reduces depression in about 85% of the people.

A psychologist said that we are all hit by the same hammer, so he made an interesting observation: "A person made three dolls, one of porcelain, one of plastic and one of steel. If you hit all three with a hammer, the porcelain would smash into pieces, the plastic one would be dented and the steel doll would give off a musical note." So, it is not the hammer but how you are made that makes the difference. Eat well, drink water, check your nutrient levels and you will be like a doll made of steel. [3]

Recommendations to Improve Nutrition:

1) Acknowledge that nutrition plays an important role in both physical and emotional wellbeing and take steps to ensure that you are moving

towards a better diet. The journey is not about perfection, but rather it is about progression. If you feel that you cannot change your diet completely, start with what you feel comfortable with - after all, some fruits and vegetables are better than none at all. I still go out and indulge in treat foods occasionally, but I am mindful about returning back to my usual healthy eating pattern soon afterwards.

2) Keep a food diary for a few days. Write down all the food that you are consuming and what impact if any, they are having on your mood. Also take note of how your body feels a few hours after the consumption of the food. Do you find yourself getting hungry often, or do you find yourself craving sweet foods after a particular meal? Do you find that you become sleepy after consuming a certain meal? Start to become aware of how your diet is affecting your daily life.

3) Educate yourself about nutrition. The following movies and documentaries may be useful: *Food Matters; Hungry for Change; Fat, Sick and Nearly Dead* and *Superjuice Me.* Also, you may want to look up the *Natural Juice Junkie* website to learn more about juicing and, also the *Gerson Institute* which is a non-profit organisation in San Diego, California, which specialises in chronic and non-toxic treatments for chronic degenerative diseases.

4) Consult a good holistic nutritionist who will be able to work with you closely on improving your nutrition.[13]

13　If you wish to contact nutritionist Deborah Colson, then please refer to the relevant reference in the bibliography where you will find her website.

In Closing

Change is necessary. The time to take responsibility for our own awakening has come. We can no longer continue to live our lives ignorant of the consequences that our actions bring. We need to question who we are; and we need to recognise the power that each of us holds to make a difference.

I do not think that we can deny any longer that we are more than what we think. The significant amount of unexplainable anecdotal evidence asks that we consider a deeper reality. It asks us to consider the existence of a Transcendent Mind.

I can only hope that my contribution through this book will help to open your heart; and provide you with hope that things can change - that you have immense strength and power; and that your existence does make a difference.

Until we meet....

BIBLIOGRAPHY

Chapter 1

[1]   Schuman, H. & Thetford, W. (2007) *A Course in Miracles.* Published by the Foundation of Inner Peace, USA. P.79.

[2]   Albery, A.P., Chandler, C., Field, A., Jones, D., Messer, D.,Moore, S. & Sterling, C., Sutton, J. & Trapp, A. (2008) *Complete Psychology.* (Second Edition) Hodder Education Publishers, London.

[3]   Buskist, W., Carlson, N.R. & Martin, G.N. (2010) *Psychology.* (Fourth Edition) Allyn & Bacon Publishers, USA.

[4]   Atkinson, R.L., Atkinson, R.C., Bem, D.J., Nolen-Hoeksema, S. & Smith, E.E. (2000) *Hilgard's Introduction to Psychology.* Harcourt Brace Publishers, USA.

[5]   Maslow, A.H. (1994) *Religion, Values and Peak Experiences.* Penguin Publishers, UK.

[6]   Quote by Max Planc. (2014) Max Planc. http://www.goodreads.com/author/quotes/107032.Max_Planck Date accessed: 14th April 2014.

Chapter 2

[1]   Quote by Einstein http://hinduism.about.com/od/thegita/a/famous-quotes.htm Date accessed: 1st April 2014.

[2]   Quote by Henry David Thoreau http://www.hinduwisdom.info/quotes1_20.htm Date accessed: 20th March 2014.

[3]   A.C Bhaktivedanta Swami Prabhupada. *Bhagavad Gita As It Is.* Publishers Krishna Books, USA.

[4]   A.C Bhaktivedanta Swami Prabhupada. *Bhagavad Gita As It Is.* Publishers Krishna Books, USA.

[5]   This story is told in chapter 3 of the Mundaka Upanishad.

[6]   This information has been taken with permission from The International Association of Near-Death Studies http://www.iands.org/about-ndes/key-nde-\facts.html?start=1 Date accessed: 06th August 2013.

[7]   This information has been taken with permission from The International Association of Near-Death Studies, http://www.iands.org/aboutndes/characteristics.html. Date accessed: 06th August 2013.

[8]   This extract/information is taken from a live interview that was conducted with Dr. Penny Sartori on 16th August 2013.

[9]   This extract/information is taken from a live interview that was conducted with Kelly Walsh on 25th September 2014.

[10]   For counter arguments about near-death experiences, please see the following book: Irwin, H.J. & Watt, C.A. *Introduction to Parapsychology.* (Fifth Edition). McFarland & Company Inc. Publishers, USA.

[11]   This extract/information is taken from a live interview with Don Oscar Miro-Quesada on 6th June 2014,

[12]   Elfferich, I., Lommel, P.V., Meyers, V. & Wees, R.V. (2001) *Near-death Experience in Survivors of Cardic Arrest: A Prospective Study in the Netherlands.* The Lancet, Volume 358. P.2039.

[13]   This extract/information was taken from an interview that was conducted by Lilou Mace on her Juicy Living Tour with Dr. Van Lommel. For more information please visit: http://www.liloumace.com/Dr-Pim-Van-Lommel-s-scientific-studies-on-near-death-experiences-and-consciousness_a2328.html Date accessed 29th August 2013.

[14]   This case study has been taken with permission from The International Association for Near-Death Studies. www.IANDS.org The full story is at http://iands.org/experiences/nde-accounts/550-met-by-mother.html.

[15]   Cooper, S. & Ring, K. (1997) *Near-Death and Out-of-Body Experiences in the Blind: A Study of Apparent Eyeless Vision.* Journal of Near-Death Studies, 16(2).

[16]   This extract/information is taken from a live interview that was conducted with Jon the 25th of April 2014.

[17]   This extract/information is taken from a live interview with Jeremy McDonald on 4th June 2014.

[18]   This extract/information is taken from a live interview that was conducted with Mercedes Leal on 07th August 2013. For more information about Mercedes please visit www.mercedesleal.com.

[19]   This extract/information was taken from an interview that was conducted by Lilou Mace on her Juicy Living Tour with Dr. Van Lommel. For more information please visit: http://www.liloumace.com/Dr-Pim-Van-Lommel-s-scientific-studies-on-near-death-experiences-and-consciousness_a2328.html Date accessed 29th August 2013.

[20]   This information has been taken from an article written by P.M.H Atwater published on The International Association for Near-Death Studies website.http://iands.org/about-ndes/common-aftereffects.html Date accessed: 16th April 2014.

Chapter 3

[1]   This extract/information is taken from a video interview that was conducted by The Institute of Noetic Sciences (IONS) with the founder of IONS, Edgar Mitchell. For more information please visit: http://noetic. org/library/video-interviews/edgar-mitchell/ Date accessed: 23rd May 2014.

[2]   This extract/information is taken from a live interview that was conducted with Cristina Klefasz Ferreira on 25th May 2014.

[3]   This extract/information is taken from a live interview that was conducted with Cristina Klefasz Ferreira on 25th May 2014.

[4]   Backster, C. (2003) *Primary Perception: Biocommunication with Plants, Living Foods and Human Cells.* White Rose Millenium Press. Anza, CA. www.primaryperception.com

[5]   Prowse, F. (2006) *Exploring a Sentient World.* Shift at The Frontiers of Consciousness. No.11. June-August (2006) pp.20-23. Date accessed May 2014.

[6]   Backster, C. Op Cit., p.29

[7]   Ibid., p.30

[8]   Ibid,. p.31

[9]   Ibid., p.32

[10]   Ibid., p.33

[11]   Ibid., p42

[12]   Quoted by permission of *Physics Essays Publication*, from *Physics Essays, Volume 7, Nr. 4, pp. 422-428 (1994).* Grinberg-Zylerbaum, J.,

Delaflor, M., Attie, L., & Goswami, A. (1994) *Einstein Podolsky Rosen Paradox in the Human Brain: The Tranferred Potential.* Physics Essays, Vol.7, pp.422-428.

[13]   Leibovici, L. (2001) *Effects of remote, retroactive, intercessory prayer on outcomes in patients with bloodstream infection: randomized controlled trial.* BMJ. Vol. 323. 22-29 December 2001.

[14]   Reprinted with permission from Mary-Ann Liebert Inc. New Rochelle, New York. Radin, D., Taft, R. & Yount, G. (2004) *Effects of Healing Intention on Cultured Cells and Truly Random Events.* The Journal of Alternative and Complimentary Medicine. Volume 10, Number 1 pp.103-112.

[15]   Radin, D., Stone, J., Levine, E., Eskandarnejad, S., Schlitz, M., Kozak, L., Mandel, D. & Hayysen, G. (2008) *Compassionate Intention as a Therapeutic Intervention by Partners of Cancer Research Patients: Effects of Distant Intention on the Patients' Autonomic Nervous System.* Explore. Volume 4, Number 4 pp. 235-243.

[16]   Quote taken from http://thinkexist.com/quotation/the_most_beautiful_thing_we_can_experience_is_the/12647.html. Date accessed 4th July 2014

[17]   Backster, C. Op Cit., p.59

[18]   This extract/information is taken from a live interview that was conducted with Dr. Dean Radin on 13th January 2014.

[19]   Schlitz, M. & Wiseman, R. (1997) *Experimenter Effects and the Remote Detection of Staring.* The Journal of Parapsychology. Vol 61. Pp.197-207

[20]   This information/extract is taken from a live interview that was conducted with Dr. Amit Goswami in May 2014.

Chapter 6

[1]   This information/extract is taken from a live interview that was conducted with Richard Flook on 1st August 2014.

[2]   Greyson, B. & Ring, K. (2004) *The Life Changes Inventory revised.* Journal of Near Death Studies 23(1). Pp. 41-54

[3]   Atwater, P.M.H (2007) *The Big Book of Near-Death Experiences: The Ultimate Guide to What Happens When We Die.* Hampton Roads Publishing, USA. pp.36-37.

Chapter 8

[1]   This extract is taken with permission from www.soulscode.com

Chapter 9

[1]   Story taken (with permission from James Colquhoun) from the *Food Matters* website: http://foodmatters.tv/content/an-interview-with-the-producer-directors-of-food-matters_ Date accessed 26th August 2014.

[2]   Story taken (with permission from Neil Martin) from the *Natural Juice Junkie* website: http://naturaljuicejunkie.com/ Date accessed 27th August 2014

[3]   Story taken with permission from The Riordan Clinic. http://orthomo-lecular.Org/library/articles/ocddepression.shtml. Date accessed 25th August 2014.

About the Author

Sunita Pattani is a Psychotherapist and Author based in East London, who specialises in exploring the link between mind, body, spirit and emotional healing. Since childhood she has been fascinated with science, spirituality, consciousness and the deeper question of who we really are. She explores this question from a multi-disciplinary perspective, and implements the findings within her therapy practice.

Pattani is a graduate of the University of Birmingham, where she obtained a degree in Mathematics, Science and Education in 2003, followed by a Postgraduate Certificate in Education (PGCE) in 2004. Pattani taught for five years before she returned to college to study an advanced diploma in Hypnotherapy and Psychotherapeutic Counselling.

Alongside running her Psychotherapy Practice, she shares her message through a combination of speaking, running workshops and writing. A regular blogger for Huffington Post, Pattani's first book, My Secret Affair with Chocolate Cake – The Emotional Eater's Guide to Breaking Free was published in 2012. Her second book The Transcendent Mind – The Missing Peace in Emotional Wellbeing is set to be published in March 2015.

In her private life Pattani practices spirituality and personal transformation. She Lives in East London, UK with her husband, Hinal and cat, Coco.

Sunita Pattani
Psychotherapist & Author.
www.sunitapattani.com
Twitter: **@sunitapattani**
Facebook: Sunita Pattani

444

07/25
07/20

7614 8270

4543 1389

Lightning Source UK Ltd.
Milton Keynes UK
UKOW02f0152080415

249282UK00001B/40/P

9 781907 989063